Integration and Change in Brazil's Middle Amazon

INTERNATIONAL
DEVELOPMENT /7

Integration and Change in Brazil's Middle Amazon

Rolf Wesche and Thomas Bruneau

University of Ottawa Press
Ottawa • London • Paris

© University of Ottawa Press, 1990
Printed and bound in Canada
ISBN 0-7766-0266-7

Canadian Cataloguing in Publication Data

Wesche, Rolf
Integration and change in Brazil's middle Amazon

(International development; 7)
Includes bibliographical references.
ISBN 0-7766-0266-7

1. Itacoatiara (Brazil) — Economic conditions.
2. Itacoatiara (Brazil) — Social conditions.
I. Bruneau, Thomas C.   II. Title.   III. Series:
International development (Ottawa, Ont.); 7.

HC189.I83W38 1990   330.981'40063   C90-090012-1

UNIVERSITÉ UNIVERSITY
D'OTTAWA OF OTTAWA

This book has been published in collaboration with the Institute for
International Development and Co-operation.

The University of Ottawa Press gratefully acknowledges the financial
assistance of the Faculty of Arts, University of Ottawa.

Design: Judith Gregory

Contents

List of Figures

List of Tables

List of Acronyms

ACAR   Associação de Crédito e Assistência Rural
       (Association for Credit and Rural Extension)

BASA   Banco da Amazônia
       (Bank of Amazonia)

BB   Banco do Brasil
       (Bank of Brazil)

BEA   Banco do Estado do Amazonas
       (Bank of the State of Amazonas)

BNDES   Banco Nacional de Desenvolvimento Econômico e
       Social
       (National Bank for Economic and Social
       Development)

CAPEMI   Caixa de Pecúlio dos Militares
       (Military Pension Fund)

CEAG-AM   Centro de Assistencia Gerencial à Pequena e Média
       Empresa do Estado do Amazonas
       (Amazonas State Centre for Management
       Assistance to Small and Medium Enterprises)

CEB   Comunidade eclesial de base
       (Basic Christian Community)

CENTREPI   Centro de Treinamento da Prelazia
       (Training Centre of the Prelacy)

CEPLAC   Comissão Executiva do Plano da Lavoura Cacaueira
       (Executive Commission of the Cacao Cultivation
       Plan)

CIMI   Conselho Indigenista Missionário
       (Native Missionary Council)

CMAI	Cooperativa Mista Agropecuária de Itacoatiara
	(Agricultural Cooperative of Itacoatiara)
CODEAGRO	Companhia de Desenvolvimento Agropecuário do Amazonas
	(Agricultural Development Company of Amazonas)
CODEAMA	Comissão de Desenvolvimento do Estado do Amazonas
	(State of Amazonas Development Commission)
CNBB	Conferéncia Nacional dos Bispos do Brasil
	(National Conference of Brazilian Bishops)
CONTAG	Confederação Nacional dos Trabalhadores na Agricultura
	(National Confederation of Rural Workers)
CPT	Conselho Pastoral da terra
	(Pastoral Land Commission)
DER-AM	Departamento de Estradas de Rodagem do Estado do Amazonas
	(Amazonas State Department of Highways)
EMATER	Empresa de Assistência Técnica e Extensao Rural
	(Agency for Technical Assistance and Rural Extension)
FINAM	Fundo para Investimentos Privados no Desenvolvimento da Amazônia
	(Fund for Private Investment in the Development of Amazonia)
IBDF	Instituto Brasileiro de Desenvolvimento Florestal
	(Brazilian Institute of Forestry Development)
IBGE	Instituto Brasileiro de Geografia e Estatística
	(Brazilian Institute of Geography and Statistics)
ICM	Imposto sobre Operacões Relativas a Circulação de Mercadorias
	(Value-added Tax)
ICOTI	Instituto de Cooperação Técnica Intermunicipal
	(Institute for Intermunicipal Technical Cooperation)
INCRA	Instituto Nacional de Colonização e Reforma Agrária
	(National Institute for Colonization and Agrarian Reform)
IPI	Imposto sobre Produtos Industrializados
	(Industrial Products Tax)
IR	Imposto de Renda
	(Income Tax)
ITERAM	Instituto de Terras do Estado do Amazonas
	(Amazonas State Land Institute)
LO	Licença de Ocupação
	(Occupation Licence)
MOBRAL	Movimento Brasileiro de Alfabetização
	(Brazilian Literacy Movement)

RADAM	Radar na Amazônia
	(Radar Mapping in Amazonia)
SEPLAN	Secretária de Estado da Coordenação do Planejamento
	(State Secretariat for Planning Coordination)
SEPROR	Secretária de Estado da Produção Rural
	(State Secretariat for Rural Production)
SESP	Serviço Especial de Sáude Pública
	(Special Public Health Service)
SPVEA	Superintendência do Plano de Valorização Econômica da Amazônia
	(Superintendency for the Amazon Economic Valorization Plan)
STR	Sindicato dos Trabalhadores Rurais
	(Rural Workers Union)
SUDAM	Superintendência do Desenvolvimento da Amazônia
	(Superintendency for the Development of Amazonia)
SUFRAMA	Superintendência da Zona Franca de Manaus
	(Superintendency of the Manaus Free-Trade Zone)

Acknowledgements

This book was initially inspired by a series of meetings between the two authors and the anthropologist Chester Gabriel, who worked in the Itacoatiara area during the early 1970s and who inspired its choice for this study. He was a member of the research team during the preparatory and field survey phase, when his familiarity with the study area proved invaluable.

In Brazil the Centro de Desenvolvimento e Planejamento Regional da Universidade Federal de Minas Gerais provided an institutional affiliation and much background on Amazon research. Its graduate students, Valeria Maria Martins Judice and Fernando Martins Prates, were competent and stimulating research assistants. Bishop George Marskell of the Prelacy of Itacoatiara provided logistical support and, more importantly, opened the doors to the extensive human network linked to the Catholic Church in Itacoatiara. We owe special gratitude to the many members of the network who provided help and hospitality, as well as to the hundreds of caboclos who shared their lives and aspirations with us.

Financial support came from the Social Sciences and Humanities Research Council of Canada and the International Development Research Center. Celia Bruneau provided much-needed editorial assistance.

INTRODUCTION

The Brazilian Amazon is a huge, underdeveloped area. In its broadest delimitation as a planning region, "Legal Amazonia" constitutes some 60 per cent of the Brazilian land mass. Characterized by a tradition of "boom and bust," with the most recent major boom caused by the extraction of raw rubber in the late nineteenth and early twentieth centuries, and a short-lived rubber boomlet during World War II, the region has been in general neglected and the population has led a tranquil and somewhat sleepy existence.

This is no longer the case, however, as the Brazilian state and economy have made major advances in incorporating the region into the national system. Yet, after twenty years of unprecedented efforts to integrate and develop the region, Legal Amazonia accounts for only 9 per cent of Brazil's population and 5 per cent of the nation's Gross National Product (GNP). The growth of the Brazilian economy and the modernization of infrastructure has provided an impetus to draw peripheral regions into the national economy. In addition, the development and elaboration of the state apparatus have made it possible to increase the control of the national bureaucracy. The motivation for this development and modernization arose from a number of interests of which the following are simply the most obvious: the need to generate foreign exchange through the export of minerals, wood products, and meat in order to promote continuing economic development and, more recently, to service the foreign debt; an awareness of declining areas (the Northeast) with excess population and of areas where agricultural modernization was displacing rural labour (the South), which encouraged the government to view the Amazon as a settlement area where the excess population could be moved and presumably absorbed; and, during the military regime (1964-85), with its pre-occupation with geopolitics and "filling empty spaces," it was considered necessary to incorporate the area administratively and militarily, not only to counter guerilla movements but also to end once and for all the perceived designs of other countries on the region.

Since 1966 and Operation Amazonia, the Brazilian state has made major efforts to incorporate the region into the larger system. These efforts have included such measures as the provision of infrastructure including roads, ports, railroads, hydro-electric complexes, and modern communications; elaborate and extensive programs of economic incentives, subsidies, and other schemes to bring capital into the area and promote economic development; and programs of planned colonization as well as other forms of settlement to increase the population of the region. These measures and their implementation are extremely important, although they have had varying degrees of success, as indicated in a number of studies (for example, Mahar 1979; Pompermayer 1979; and Skillings and Tcheyan 1979).

The region and the process of change it is undergoing have attracted the attention of a broad spectrum of physical and social scientists

1

not only because of these economic and administrative measures formulated and implemented by the government, but also because of their impact in conjunction with other political and economic processes. Initially a certain mystery surrounded this huge and diverse region encompassing the world's largest remaining tropical rain forest, for which there are few reliable data on the varied and complex ecology. The impact on the ecology as rivers are dammed, forests cleared, and new crops introduced is still a matter for polemic as much as it is for scientific study, since the ecological implications are not limited to Brazil but may well have a climatic impact in other parts of the world (for example, Potter 1975; Fearnside 1985). The long-term implications of change in the Amazon ecology will undoubtedly be studied, discussed, and debated for decades, if not centuries. Attention has also been focused on the more immediate impact of change on indigenous and settler populations in the area, as this process has generated considerable violence (CNBB 1977; Souza Martins 1980; Carvalho 1980). Indians have been moved from one area to another, suffered from diseases and alcoholism after contact with settlers, at times fought back, and, in many cases, have simply disintegrated as tribal entities. *Posseiros* (squatters) with some claim to the land they occupy have frequently been forcefully removed when large enterprises, usually from the State of São Paulo or abroad, buy the land and clear away forest and existing occupants. Increasingly the posseiros are fighting back and there is a spiral of violence. Even the process of planned colonization has resulted in a human drama as people have moved into the Amazon only to find that the land is unsuitable for agriculture, not easily accessible to roads, or that the prices for crops are insufficient to cover costs. The conflicts and violence have not gone unnoticed. Not only have the state and important economic interests become deeply involved, but so have other organizations and groups, national and international. These include organizations affiliated with the Catholic Church (CPT and CIMI), unions, political parties, and international groups such as Cultural Survival and the World Wildlife Fund.

This interest has increasingly become focused in social science research on the process of incorporation and change in the Amazon area. During the past decade a respectable body of research has emerged as Brazilians and other social scientists have studied the region and published their findings. The References Cited include some key contributions in this expanding field of study. It should be noted that the majority of this research has been conducted either in areas of planned colonization or where the abruptness of incorporation and change have resulted in high levels of violence. These areas are primarily on the southern and eastern fringes of the Amazon where roads have opened up sparsely settled or uninhabited *terra firme* (interfluve) lands in the last twenty years. In contrast, the riverine zones of the Amazon River and its major tributaries, which contain most of Amazonia's traditional population, have received limited attention (for example, Bunker 1981, 1984; Lima 1956; Parker 1981, 1985; Sternberg 1956). Several studies have been exclusively historical (for example, Sweet 1974; Weinstein 1980).

The contribution of the present study rests on its broad analysis of the social impact of contemporary development in a riverine area which differs in many ways from the terra firme frontiers which have attracted the bulk of previous research attention. As Moran (1981) has argued, it is necessary to be aware of the many, diverse Amazons (xiv:7) because it is difficult to generalize from one area to another. Rather, one should focus on specific cases or areas, while bearing in mind the findings from research on other cases and areas. What is specific about the municipality of Itacoatiara in the Middle Amazon is its early settlement and previous slow rate of change. Located in a strategic region below the confluence of the Amazon and Madeira rivers (Figure 1), the town was established in its present location in 1759, gaining *cidade* (city) status in 1874 (SUDAM 1970:13). Since 1965 it has been linked by road with the state capital, Manaus, which, in 1967, was designated a *Zona Franca* (Free Trade Zone), with the objective of serving as a growth centre to stimulate the regional development of the middle and western Amazon (Mahar 1976). By 1978 the road was paved and a number of feeder roads extended into the immediate hinterland of the town. This municipality, then, has been incorporated into the larger Brazilian system for longer than the colonization frontiers which are most frequently studied. There have been no major discoveries of minerals or promising terra firme soils in the area, nor have major colonization schemes been proposed. Most of the areas which have been studied are terra firme. Itacoatiara has approximately 30 per cent of its land in *varzeas* (floodplains) in the middle course of the Amazon, with good soils characterized by regular flooding. The rest of the municipality is composed of generally poor terra firme soils (DNPM 1976). There are three distinct zones in the municipality: (1) the City of Itacoatiara, which, in 1980, had slightly more than half of the municipality's 52,882 inhabitants (IBGE 1980c); (2) the river zone, composed of floodplain and adjacent terra firme fringe; and (3) the terra firme road zone (Figure 2). The river zone contains three-quarters and the road zone one-quarter, of the rural population.

Although Itacoatiara has not seen the ''nothing to something'' pattern of frontier development of other parts of the Amazon, it has nonetheless increasingly entered into the same process of incorporation. Infrastructure has been established; for example, the paved road, a new port, and the provision and continual upgrading of services such as water, electricity and communications. State and federal governments provide facilities through numerous agencies and banks. Credit and incentives for agricultural and industrial products have been extended. Today, the paved road to the state capital, infrastructure, and other elements of modern Brazil make the municipality something of a regional growth centre, based on its role as an entrepot and its substantial and growing wood-processing industry. In sum, although the municipality may have started from a more developed level than much of the Amazon, the last ten years have seen it become increasingly incorporated into the larger Brazilian political and economic system, along with its ''frontier'' counterparts.

FIGURE 1   *Itacoatiara: Location and Hinterland*

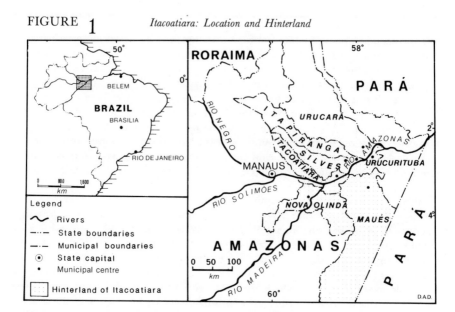

FIGURE 2   *Municipality of Itacoatiara: Environmental Zones*

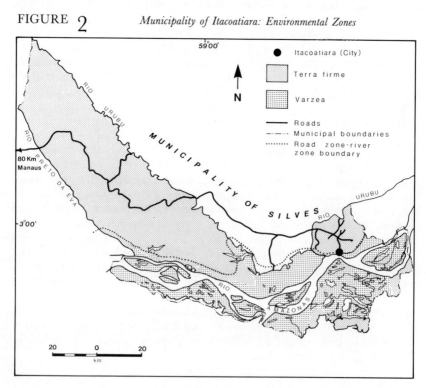

Our purpose in the research project is to evaluate the nature of change in the municipality in the period from 1970 to 1980. We will describe the area in the base period, indicate what kinds of new or old actors came to operate in the area, discuss the impact on the population—particularly in regard to credit facilities, changing land tenure arrangements, and employment generation—and indicate how the population has responded to its changing situation. We hope to make our findings from the research in one area relevant to studies in other areas. By highlighting some of the common themes, we will now set the basic parameters.

First. All studies of the social impact of development in the Amazon must be eclectic and, it is hoped, interdisciplinary. The region is huge, and environmental factors, many of which constrain development, are extremely important. These factors are responsible for the area's low population and slight contribution to the country's GNP. Until recently land, much of it poor land, was for the taking, and settlements were scattered and very small. The differentiation and elaboration of groups, let alone classes, was low. Now, as political, economic, and communication structures of modern Brazil penetrate the region, a sense of very rapid change—and at times of tragedy—is apparent. It is difficult to capture all these elements, yet all must be taken into consideration, because a close relationship exists between the ecology, human settlement, agriculture, and economic and political processes. On the one hand, one can comprehend the processes at work in modern Brazil by examining these smaller, relatively distant and isolated areas, and analyzing their dynamics. On the other, it must be recognized that, in the analysis of these frontier areas, the physical environment plays a paramount role. Through interdisciplinary work one can hope to achieve a synthesis of the various factors involved in the nature and impact of change.

Our study team included an anthropologist with experience in this area in the early 1970s, a geographer who had worked on colonization schemes and the establishment of road networks, and a political scientist with experience in the study of state structures and the Catholic Church. We collected all available data from government sources—such as IBGE, CODEAMA, ICOTI—as well as documentation on the area by individuals and groups. The three principal investigators conducted interviews in the municipality and in Manaus with political figures, government officials, economic leaders, and members of the Church, unions, and cooperatives. Central to the study is a sample survey of 575 heads of household (almost seven per cent of the area's population) conducted in 1981 with a questionnaire which included items on a variety of demographic, economic, social, religious, and political variables (Survey 1981). There was also a survey of most of the major economic establishments which were operational in 1981 (Elite Survey 1981). The area was revisited by one member of the research team in November 1985 to identify any significant changes. The project is, then, interdisciplinary and broad based, as is appropriate for a study of the social impact of development.

5

Second. Regardless of the disciplinary basis of researchers on Amazonian development, explicit attention must be given to the role of the state. The region has been underdeveloped, isolated, and neglected, largely because of environmental factors which make life very difficult. In addition, few economic benefits have been derived from the area, with the exception of the boom and bust of the rubber era and a few specific crops such as cacao, Brazil nuts, and pepper. The state has been the prime mover in promoting the incorporation and economic development of the area and has mobilized resources for infrastructure, economic incentives, and a variety of programs. As Wagley argues (1984:ix), it is simply impossible to neglect the role of the state in promoting integration of the Amazon. Mahar (1979) describes government policies and analyzes their general impact. Pompermayer (1979) shows how private enterprise pressures the government for policies which make involvement and investment in the Amazon attractive for large entrepreneurs. And Bunker (1985) gives particular attention to the role of ideology and of bureaucratic dynamics in determining the precise role of the state, showing how processes of change, mainly to the detriment of the peasants, are hastened by state involvement in infrastructure and incentives. It should be noted that all of the policies and programs which were analyzed were formulated and implemented during the period of military rule with its emphasis on economic growth and national security. It is valid to ask whether this role will be any different in the present context of civilian government with its rhetoric of change and social reform.

Third. All of the social scientists, and many of the physical scientists, researching in the Amazon are not interested in the administrative and economic policies per se but rather in terms of their impact on people. The region is characterized by very low population density, little natural infrastructure, primarily subsistence agriculture and some forest extraction for export, and little legal apparatus in such areas as land tenure and fishing rights. Government policies and economic involvement have initiated a process of rapid penetration and inclusion in the rest of Brazil. What is the impact of this process? This is the question most often asked in the research on the Amazon.

Most frequently the impact of the process of inclusion is examined through the impact on land tenure arrangements because a large part of the population in the region is rural. Most studies on the Amazon region indicate that the overall result of penetration and inclusion is to concentrate land holdings among a few owners, with negative impact on the rural agricultural population. Foweraker (1981) shows how dispossession of the peasantry is not exclusive to recent development in the Amazon, but has been significant in other parts of Brazil and during other periods. Bunker (1985:237) demonstrates how penetration overwhelms local society: land increases in value because of government subsidies and the construction of infrastructure, and, whereas land tenure was not previously an issue, it becomes a matter for juridical definitions in the modern state. Even Skillings and Tcheyan (1979), in what is generally a sanguine discussion of the process of Amazonian development, raise serious questions about the land tenure situation. Sawyer (1984) also demonstrates how large private interests concentrate land holding but he, as others, raises the question of whether this is productive use of land or simply a means to obtain economic incentives from the state and a hedge against inflation. Taken as a whole, with the possible exception of Moran (1981) social scientists paint a bleak picture of the land tenure situation and its impact on the agricultural population. Wagley (1984:xii) epitomizes the situation in a suggestion that the process is recreating in the Amazon region the classic *latifundia-minifundia* dichotomy of much of the rest of Brazil.

Itacoatiara is going through some of these processes—albeit not as rapidly or as dramatically as in such areas as Pará or Mato Grosso. Outsiders and local business interests, with government incentives and credit, have been buying land, although as late as 1981 there was still not a serious local land shortage. Possibly on the floodplain the growing of jute helped to consolidate land tenure. However, as shall be seen, this also entailed indebtedness which could result in the loss of land. Further, the road area has shown some indications of a shortage of land, and some data suggest that peasants have been forced to move because of a lack of land. In sum, while not as obvious or dramatic as in some areas of the Amazon there is evidence of the same processes of land concentration and subsequent land shortage for the lowest classes.

Fourth. In this study some attention is given to the role of organized actors, such as the Church and unions, which have resisted the trend towards land concentration. Bunker (1985) and Souza Martins (1981, 1984) have dealt with this topic, but it is probably Pompermayer (1979) who has given it the most explicit attention. In most of the areas studied, however, organized resistance developed primarily after the process of land concentration was fairly well advanced. As the hope of the peasants declined, the level of violence increased. In the municipality of Itacoatiara, not only has the process of inclusion and subsequent land concentration been slower, but a greater basis for organizing resistance has been apparent. The Catholic Church is particularly important in this process and plays a crucial role in encouraging the formation of cooperatives and urban and rural unions. Thus it would seem that the peasants of Itacoatiara stand a better chance of retaining their hold on the land than those in most other parts of the Amazon. If resistance to land concentration fails here because of cultural factors such as passivity and lack of awareness, it will probably not work anywhere unless a major structural change occurs during the present political transition from a military to a civilian regime. In spite of announcements of land reform, this change seems unlikely.

1. ITACOATIARA IN 1970

Before the new road to Manaus opened the way to change around 1970, Itacoatiara in many ways fitted the stereotype of municipalities along the Amazon River. It was large, though near the lower end of the municipal size range in the Brazilian Amazon, with a surface area of 6,727 square kilometres (SUDAM 1970:13). It was thinly populated, though near the upper end of the municipal density range in the Brazilian Amazon, with 5.6 inhabitants per square kilometre. It was divided into three distinct units: (a) the city of Itacoatiara; (b) the river zone, which encompasses the Amazon and its backwaters, the extensive varzea, and a narrow terra firme fringe adjacent to river or varzea; and (c) the terra firme interior (Figure 2). Most of the rural settlement and economic activity was concentrated in the river zone, traditionally advantaged in terms of transportation and resource endowment. Meanwhile, the terra firme interior, with soils classed as poor or very poor for agriculture (DNPM 1976) and with no notable resources other than its forest cover, remained virtually untouched.

THE CITY

A sharp division existed between the municipality's single urban centre—more like an oversized village with a few imposing structures dating from the rubber period—and the rural hinterland, which was devoid of infrastructure except for a few primary schools. Itacoatiara had achieved *cidade* status in 1874 (SUDAM 1970:13, SEPLAN 1980b:3), shortly after the beginning of the rubber period. It was the first settlement after the state capital to be so honoured, an indication of the city's early importance. With 15,881 inhabitants in 1970, it remained the state's second largest city after Manaus, which, with a population of 312,160, was about twenty times larger.

In 1970, 43 per cent of the municipal census population of 37,346 was urban. This relatively high level of urbanization for a traditional society based on the primary sector conforms to the predominant pattern of excessive urbanization in Amazonia,[1] where 1970 state-level urbanization

---

1. Where statistics are given for Amazonia, also referred to as "the region," they apply, unless otherwise specified, to the North region of the Brazilian census which comprises the present states of Acre, Amazonas, Pará, Rondônia, and the federal territories of Amapá and Roraima. This area, often referred to as "Traditional Amazonia," forms the bulk of the modern planning region "Legal Amazonia," which also includes parts of Goiás, Mato Grosso, and Maranhão.

rates range from 28 per cent in Acre to 54 per cent in Amapá (Mahar 1979:37). The 42 per cent rate for Amazonas (IBGE 1970b) roughly matches that of Itacoatiara. Most of Amazonia's urban population have always lived in the state capitals; in 1970 Belém and Manaus alone accounted for almost 90 per cent of the region's urban population (Mahar 1979:37). If state capitals are excluded from an intermunicipal comparison, Itacoatiara's proportion of urban population in 1970 appears extraordinarily high.

This is largely attributable to the city's strategic location. Not only is Itacoatiara located on the main thoroughfare of Amazonia, the heavily travelled portion of the Amazon River below Manaus, but it is also situated near the confluence with the Madeira River, which, for over a century, was the Amazon's most important tributary in economic terms. Thus Itacoatiara's geographical location rivaled that of Manaus.

Due to this advantageous location, Itacoatiara functioned as the service centre of seven municipalities[2] (Figure 1), with a combined population in 1970 of 97,269. Itacoatiara was recognized as one of five subregional centres[3] below the level of Manaus in Amazonas state's classification of the urban hierarchy (SEPLAN 1989a). In addition to its role within the immediate hinterland, Itacoatiara served as a processing and transshipment centre for lumber, rubber, and Brazil nuts from remote upriver locations in the Amazon and Madeira watersheds.

Itacoatiara's high urban ratio also reflected the absence of infrastructure and services in the countryside. And, as elsewhere in Amazonia, the uprooting fluctuations of the primary export economy, floods, and the extreme concentration of municipal and economic opportunity in the city have tended to encourage rural-urban migration.

However, the 1970 urbanization rate of 43 per cent suggests a higher degree of urban characteristics than actually existed. Only 33 per cent of the municipality's economically active population worked in the secondary and tertiary sectors (Table 1). This indicates that a large proportion of urban residents were employed in the primary sector, including agriculture, within walking and canoe distance of the city, while only an insignificant percentage of rural residents worked outside the primary sector. Virtually the entire secondary and tertiary sectors were traditional and small scale.

The secondary sector contained 10.6 per cent of the labour force in 1970 (Table 1). It must be assumed, however, that the vast majority of these workers were engaged in cottage industries and simple construction—activities which would largely be classified as part of the informal sector. Only nine establishments had a workforce of five or more persons (Table 2). All these businesses were involved in low-technology processing of local or regional raw materials.

The six major export-oriented enterprises confined themselves to the minimum processing required to make products ready for shipment.

---

2. These include Itacoatiara, Itapiranga, Maués, Nova Olinda do Norte, Silves, Urucará, and Urucurituba.
3. The other subregional centres are Parintins, Tefé, Benjamin Constant, and Eirunepé.

TABLE 1   *Economically Active Population of the Municipality by Sector of Employment, 1970*

	Number of Persons	Percentage of Labour Force
Primary sector	6,266	67.5
Secondary sector	981	10.6
Tertiary sector	2,032	21.9
Commerce	499	5.4
Services	573	6.2
Transport, communication, storage	301	3.2
Social activities	443	4.8
Public administration	111	1.2
Other	105	1.1
Total	9,279	100.0

Source: IBGE 1970b.

TABLE 2   *Industrial Establishments with Five or More Workers, 1970*

Name (Year of foundation)	Ownership L = local[a] E = external	Main products
Brasiljuta (1962)	E	jute, cacao
I.B. Sabba (1955)	E	jute, Brazil nuts, sorva, rosewood
Cooperativa Mista (1968)	L	jute, various crops
Correia Indústria e Comercio (1954) (Correia)	L	jute, Brazil nuts, cacao
Itacoatiara Industrial (1952)	E	lumber
Usina Cecy (1955) (Chibly)	L	rubber
Olaria Sto Antonio (1955)	L	bricks
Guaranà Rio Negro (1953) (Mamede)	L	soft drinks
Matadouro Municipal (1920)	L	meat

Source: Elite Survey, CEAG-AM no date
[a]For locally owned family firms, the surname of the principal owner appears in parentheses.

Four enterprises specializing in jute and, to a lesser extent, cacao, Brazil nuts, sorva and rosewood, were essentially sorting, baling, drying and storage operations; they did not involve any significant transformation of products. Two mills produced sawn lumber, part of which was used for local construction. The single rubber factory converted rubber bales into pressed sheets. A bottling plant produced a guaraná softdrink for local and regional consumption. The two brick factories exclusively served the local market. None of these operations required skilled labour, and the majority of their labour force suffered seasonal unemployment because of fluctuations in the supply of raw materials.

Private enterprise in the tertiary sector was almost totally characterized by a proliferation of small-scale activities. Commerce, for example, was represented by 245 establishments in 1970 (SUDAM 1970:26), averaging two workers per establishment. Among this welter of small-scale activity, however, two wholesale-retail trading houses stood out, not because of their importance as employers, but because of their central role in the trading system of the region. These were the family businesses Irmãos Mamede and Ipenor Menezes (Table 3). The former dates back to the rubber period. They functioned as the major importers of consumer goods and agricultural production inputs, wholesale suppliers to the urban retailers and rural traders, and retail sales points for urban and rural customers. They provided informal credit and purchased and resold primary products. As purveyors of credit in return for raw materials, they had much in common with the "industries" handling jute and extractive products, which were trading houses as much as manufacturing establishments.

TABLE 3   *Commercial Establishments with Five or More Workers, 1970*

Name (Year of foundation)	Ownership L = local[a] E = external	Main Products
Irmãos Mamede (1908) (Mamede)	L	general merchandise
Ipenor Menezes (1963) (Menezes)	L	general merchandise
Chibly Cia Terminal de Petroleo (Chibly)	L	petroleum products

Source: Elite Survey.
[a]For locally owned family firms, the surname of the principal owner appears in parentheses.

Of the government services and infrastructure, only the primary education system, staffed by 243 poorly trained teachers, had penetrated the countryside. Fifty-eight of the municipality's ninety-two primary schools were in the rural areas, and the rural attendance rate among the school-age population was close to the municipal mean of 67 per cent (SUDAM 1970:29-30).

Two traditionalist secondary schools, one public, the other Catholic, as well as the adult education movement MOBRAL, functioned in the city, with only one of the thirty-one secondary school teachers holding the appropriate diploma (SUDAM 1970:30). Health services were even more rudimentary; a total of four doctors operated a small Catholic hospital and two health posts of SESP. The majority of deaths occurred without medical attention (SUDAM 1970:31). A further indication of the low quality of life in the city was the limited percentage of households with public water (36 per cent), electricity (48 per cent), garbage collection (40 per cent), and telephone (0.8 per cent) (SUDAM 1970:37-41). Only the main roads were paved, and the 2,000 metre-long sewage system had only 200 connections.

The demands of modern economic development were served by three banks: the Banco do Brasil (BB), the Banco da Amazonia S.A. (BASA), and the Banco do Estado do Amazonas S.A. (BEA). However, they offered only limited and constantly changing lines of credit, primarily for commerce and medium and large agricultural enterprises. The city's power supply was modest; in 1969 it had been upgraded to three generators totalling 2328 kw and was prone to frequent breakdowns (SUDAM 1970:39-40).

Perhaps the most critical obstacles to economic expansion were the inadequate systems of transportation and communication. The primitive public dock had sunk. Thus even small boats had difficulty landing, and steamers had to tie up at the precarious *trapiches* (docks) of a sawmill and two jute exporters. Manaus, though only 283 km away by the newly opened dirt road and even less by river, still seemed rather remote: the daily bus and thrice weekly riverboat took between eight and sixteen hours. The probability of long waits on the four interurban telephone circuits helps to explain the modest daily average of 490 interurban calls in 1970 (SUDAM 1970:39). Thus the once-daily DC-3 Cruzeiro do Sul flight to Manaus remained a vital lifeline.

THE RURAL AREA

If modernization was delayed in the city of Itacoatiara, it was even slower in the river zone, which, until the late 1960s, accommodated most of the rural population. Here, long-established patterns of adaptation to the physical environment and to the demands of the primary export economy prevailed. The river zone, if seen as a complementary system of water bodies—varzea and adjoining terra firme fringe—represents a relatively rich and highly diversified resource endowment.[4] This applies particularly to the Middle Amazon, in which Itacoatiara is located, where the varzea reaches a width of up to 100 kilometres.

---

4. A number of observers of modern frontier expansion in the Brazilian Amazon have called for a shift of (at least agricultural) development emphasis from terra firme to varzea agriculture (e.g., Barrow 1985, Smith 1982). However, the river zone has severe environmental shortcomings which are increasingly perceived by local residents as constraints in the face of the new demands and expectations of a modernizing society.

Life in the river zone of the Middle Amazon is, of course, determined above all by the river, which provides transport and fertility and controls the seasonal cycle of human activity. With its numerous branches and connected lakes, the river forms an extensive natural transportation network and, until the late 1960s, represented virtually the only means of transportation. This network varies dramatically with the seasons. During the flood season, when the area under water may triple (Smith 1981:11), most of the varzea and terra firme fringe is accessible by canoe, if not by river boat, while overland transport in the varzea is correspondingly restricted. In contrast, during the low-water season, many of the lesser water bodies and shorelines become so shallow or clogged with vegetation as to impede navigation. Thus only limited areas in the river zone have assured year-round access.

The sediment load of the Amazon derives from the Andean watershed, like that of all of its "whitewater" tributaries. This sediment accounts for a rich aquatic life as well as the fertility of the floodplain. There is no doubt that predatory exploitation of the aquatic fauna since the beginning of European occupation has sharply reduced some species which were easily hunted and in high demand such as manatees, turtles, and alligators as well as some fish species, particularly the pirarucú. Yet in 1970, fish was still easily caught and provided most of the animal protein consumed by the riverine population, both rural and urban. When floods made fish difficult to harvest, animals which gathered on high ground helped to supplement the protein diet.

Soil fertility in the varzea, though varied, is generally much superior to that of Itacoatiara's terra firme. A further advantage of varzea soils for a traditional agriculture emphasizing diversification, though a potential constraint for modern agriculture, is their considerable heterogeneity in terms of physical, chemical, and drainage characteristics. These are a function of relative exposure to the main river channel and variations in the microtopography which determine the nature of sedimentation as well as frequency and duration of flooding. Not only is the river "the plow" (Higbee 1945), manipulating the soils and helping to control spontaneous vegetation, but it also serves to reduce insect pests, plant pathogens and, in some island locations, even the rodent population. Finally it should be noted that the Middle Amazon benefits from greater river channel stability than exists in the upper watershed and so erosion and spatial change of the varzea land surface and terra firme embankments is not a major problem (Denevan 1984; Parker 1981).

However, there are great irregularities in the timing and amplitude of the annual flood, which, in conjunction with the duration of the low-water period, are the main determinants of agricultural risk and annual production in the varzea. In the absence of long-term data for Itacoatiara, this problem is best illustrated by measurements near the junction of the Amazon and Negro rivers, some 200 kilometres upstream from Itacoatiara (Figures 3 and 4). Furthermore, Itacoatiara's varzea areas are located below the mouth of the Negro River and around the mouth of the Madeira, that is, near the Amazon's junction with its two most voluminous tributaries, which have their own irregularities and roughly opposite seasonal cycles. Thus the local river regime is particularly complex and unpredictable; although it obeys the general annual cycle of the Middle Amazon with a single flood season, it may have more than one crest (Figure 3). In the varzea, only one annual crop planted on higher or intermediate elevations following the receding waters is completely free of flood risk. Even mature tree crops on the highest ground of the Itacoatiara varzea area are severely damaged by extreme floods, that is, floods cresting higher than twenty-nine metres above sea level (Figure 4). These have occurred on average once every ten years from 1903 to 1976 (IBGE 1977:116).

FIGURE 3
Frequency of Maximum and Minimum Levels of the Amazon River near Its Confluence with the Negro River, by Month, 1903-1973

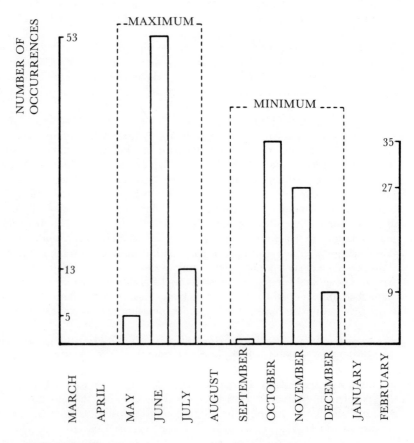

Source: IBGE 1977: 110.

FIGURE 4   *Maximum and Minimum Levels of the Negro River at Manaus, 1902–1973*

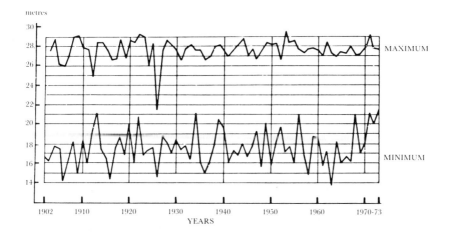

Source: IBGE 1977: 115.

    The varzea has dominated crop production in Itacoatiara, both in acreage and volume. This is particularly due to the considerable width of the varzea belt in this area and the fact that an adequate supply of varzea land was available to support the existing population. The staple crops for subsistence and the local market were manioc, beans, maize, sweet potatoes, and plantain. Cacao, which was grown on the higher ground of the *varzea alta* was traditionally the dominant export crop.

    After 1934, when Japanese settlers introduced jute to the area, the relative importance of cacao declined. Jute proved particularly adaptable to natural flooding and simple agricultural techniques, which explains its wide acceptance by the local population.[5] The 1960s saw the introduction of malva, another fibre crop with greater productivity per area unit. Although no reliable statistics exist, it seems clear that, in the varzea of Itacoatiara in the late 1960s, jute and malva exceeded the acreage of all other crops combined.

    The terra firme fringe, the third component of the river zone, combines the advantages of easy access to river and varzea, flood protection, good air circulation, and surface drainage. It is relatively free from the seasonal blackfly infestation of large parts of the varzea. Embankments are lined with extensive bands of anthropogenic *terra preta* (black anthropogenic soils) of considerable fertility (Smith 1980), suggesting that there is a long tradition to the local preference for settling on terra firme embankments.

---

5. Furthermore, it had an assured national market because of the coffee industry's growing demand for jute bags and the prohibition of jute imports in 1947 (Oliveira 1983:262).

Some food crops were grown on the terra firme fringe, among which manioc was by far the most important. The terra firme fringe was also used for small stands of tree crops, particularly cacao and rubber, the latter based on seedstock from the local forest. It was also the main site of lumber extraction, as well as Brazil nut gathering and rubber tapping in the natural forest. These last two activities occasionally involved incursions into the terra firme interior.

Extractive activities, however, were of little local significance in terms of employment, and declined with the expansion of jute cultivation. For example, because the most accessible timber had already been cut, the traders and processing plants of Itacoatiara depended on more distant municipalities for their supply of extractive products.

The traditional symbiotic relationship between the three areas of the river zone is best illustrated by the transfer of livestock from the varzea to the terra firme fringe during the flood season, the crucial role of terra firme manioc and game during the food shortages which affect the varzea in the latter part of and shortly after the annual flood, and the daily commuting by foot or canoe between terra firme residence and varzea farmland. These are only some illustrations of the fact that rural society, in 1970 still essentially confined to the river zone, depended on the integrated use of its diversified and complementary resource endowment, and that many *caboclos* (peasants) were individually drawing subsistence or income from all three components of this environment.

This is not to suggest that, before 1970, inhabitants either maximized the sustainable yield of the riverine environment or sought stability through maximum diversification of resource use. Rather, there was a well-established tendency to focus excessively on export products, particularly when they commanded high prices, and to neglect food production accordingly. Thus, though surrounded by an underutilized agricultural hinterland, Itacoatiara imported food staples such as *farinha*, the coarse flour derived from manioc, as well as beans and rice. The range of agricultural products in the city's three open markets was meagre and few fresh vegetables were available.

CREDIT AND TRADE

The principal system organizing the local primary export economy and linking city and hinterland was a variant of the hierarchical debt dependency which prevailed throughout traditional Amazonia. This system exploited the peasantry while providing it with some protection against such catastrophes as floods and commodity price collapse, since the intermediaries depended on the continuation of the peasantry. In the most common form of this system, the commercial houses and primary product-processing establishments in Itacoatiara provided informal credit and supplies to rural traders who in turn supplied a network of dependent peasants. Most of the rural traders were based in the countryside, generally were themselves engaged in agriculture or livestock raising, and dealt with peasants in the vicinity of their rural residence. In addition, a small number of *regatões* (itinerant river traders), dealt with a more dispersed clientele. These intermediaries channelled primary export products from the peasants to the trading houses and processors in Itacoatiara. In this system each *patrão* (patron) attempted to monopolize the export products of his clients. The client, particularly the peasant, depended on the assured credit and guaranteed market which a stable tie to a single individual provided.

Several factors contributed, however, to reducing the rigidity of this system and to inhibiting excessive exploitation of the peasant, particularly if one compares the local situation to the extreme exploitation of the *aviamento* system of the rubber period, when remoteness, control of supplies, output, and the land resource by an intermediary, the tendency of the intermediary to impede subsistence production (Ross 1978), and lack of state protection for the rubber gatherer conspired to keep the caboclo in a condition approaching slavery.

First, the rural caboclo population of Itacoatiara was essentially composed of peasants who controlled the land which they worked, even though legal titles were virtually unknown. In 1970, 92 per cent of the 2,584 farms[6] in Itacoatiara were classified as owner operated. If one uses the average rural family size for Amazonas of 5.6 persons (IBGE 1970b) and if one assumes, somewhat arbitrarily, that all owner-operators were rural residents, 62 per cent of the 1970 rural census population would consist of the families of owner-operators. In the absence of appropriate employment statistics, the percentage of establishments involved in the production of various primary export products sheds some light on the likely extent of control of large landowners over dependent labourers in the primary export sector (Table 4).

TABLE 4   *Rural Establishments Reporting Export Products in 1970*

Establishments reporting:	jute	1,418	(54.9%)
	cacao	475	(18.4%)
	rubber	98	(3.8%)
	Brazil nuts	3	(0.1%)
	lumber	3	(0.1%)
Total establishments		2,584	(100.0%)

Source: IBGE 1970a.

Jute and cacao, both overwhelmingly produced on family farms, clearly dominated. Extractive products such as lumber, rubber, and Brazil nuts were of limited significance. Furthermore, most of the establishments reporting rubber were small farms on which planted stands of rubber

6. The term "farm" is used as synonymous to "estabelecimento agropecuário" which Brazil's 1980 census defines as a "continuous area subordinated to a single producer" under any form of tenure and used for agriculture and/or extraction from the natural vegetation (IBGE 1980b:14). Few farms in Itacoatiara are exclusively or predominantly devoted to extractive activities.

were tapped by family labour. Thus, even if some establishments with extrac-tive products in remote locations were neglected during the enumeration of the 1970 census, it is evident that the amount of hired labour engaged in extrac-tive activities on large concessions or estates was quite limited.

A second factor reducing the control by intermediaries was the existence of competition, not only among local processors and trading houses and among local rural traders and regatoes, but also between regatoes based in Manaus and down-river ports. When commodity prices of the raw mate-rials ran high, competition increased and the regatoes worked larger areas than usual. Particularly along the most heavily travelled waterways, peasants had access to a variety of outlets for their export products. They tended to use them with discretion, however, to maintain the goodwill of their patrões.

Third, most peasants were at least partially diversified pro-ducers. Subsistence production from crop agriculture, fishing, and hunting reduced their requirements of purchased food. Surpluses from these subsist-ence activities could also be marketed with little interference from the patrão, because of the latter's tendency to specialize in export products.

Although these factors helped to control exploitation by middle-men, the peasants had no escape from dependence. They lacked the sizable motor-powered boats required to move the bulky jute bales, and the major-ity of them lived too far away from the city to reach it by canoe. Further-more, though the Banco do Brasil had operated in Itacoatiara since 1952, peasant access to bank credit remained difficult because of distance and com-plex administrative requirements, lack of appropriately targeted credit pro-grams, and the absence of land titles. The availability of bank credit to the intermediaries meant that they could expand the range of goods and services they could offer to their clients. Finally, life for the varzea population, in par-ticular those lacking access to terra firme cropland, is essentially an annual cycle of feast and famine in which food shortages at the end of the flood season (possibly compounded by flood damage and illness), leave the varzea peasant vulnerable to the intermediary.

LAND TENURE

In this traditional system where social control and stratifica-tion were based on commerce and informal credit, the skewed land tenure (Table 5) played a minor role in the lives of the inhabitants and was not an important social issue. In 1970, 86 per cent of farms fell below the 100 hectare limit, which was then considered the minimum size for a viable family farm in the Brazilian Amazon; however, there was no noticeable land shortage. A large proportion of the smaller farms were located in the varzea, where five hectares of better land under crops provided an adequate living for a family and where it would be difficult to cultivate a larger area under annual crops with only family labour, given the timing constraints imposed by the annual flood cycle. A comparison of data on land tenure and area per farm under crops (Tables 5 and 6) clearly indicates a gross underutilization of land

TABLE 5   *Farms and Area in Farms by Size Category, 1970*

Farm Size (hectares)	Number of Farms	Percentage of Total Farms	Total Farm Land (hectares)	Percentage of Total Farm Land	Mean Size of Farm (hectares)
Up to 4.9	435	16.8	1,134	0.8	2.6
5 - 9.9	386	14.9	2,582	1.8	6.7
10 - 24.9	563	21.8	7,494	5.1	13.3
25 - 49.9	617	23.9	16,648	11.4	27.0
50 - 99.9	223	8.6	13,963	9.6	62.6
100 - 199	156	6.0	19,161	13.1	122.8
200 - 499	154	6.0	39,165	26.9	234.3
500 - 999	33	1.3	19,271	13.2	584.0
1000 and over	17	0.7	26,477	18.1	1,557.5
Total	**2,584**	**100.0**	**145,895**	**100.0**	**56.5**

Source: Based on IBGE 1970a.

TABLE 6   *Farms by Area under Crops, 1970*

Area under crops (hectares)	Number of Farms	Percentage of Farms
0	97	3.8
0.1 - 0.9	96	3.7
1 - 1.9	596	23.1
2 - 4.9	1,415	54.8
5 - 9.9	331	12.8
10 - 19.9	41	1.6
20 - 49.9	5	0.2
50 - 99.9	1	0.0
100 - 200	2	0.1
Total	**2,584**	**100.1[a]**

Source: Based on IBGE 1970a.
[a]Totals more than 100 per cent because of rounding.

among small as well as large farms, even taking into consideration the large proportion of varzea land unsuited to crop cultivation and the need for land rotation on the terra firme. The low mean area of 2.4 hectares under temporary crops per farm (Table 7) confirms this pattern. Since peasants were frequently unable to use or uninterested in using all their farm land, a number of informal arrangements existed among the peasants to accommodate the landless population, often with only token compensation to the landholder.

TABLE 7   *Land Use of Farms, 1970*

	Number of Farms[a]	Percentage of Total Farms	Total Farm Land (hectares)	Percentage of Total Farm Land	Mean Area per Farm (hectares)
Annual crops	2,413	93.4	5,732	3.9	2.4
Perennial crops	1,185	45.9	1,957	1.3	1.7
Natural pasture	751	29.1	10,277	7.0	13.7
Planted pasture	515	19.9	7,470	5.1	14.5
Forest, fallow, unused	2,584	100.0	120,458	82.7	46.6
Total of farms/area	2,584	100.0	145,894	100.0	

Source: Based on IBGE 1970a
[a]Note multiple counting because a farm may contain several land use categories.

Furthermore, the 1970 census indicates that the majority of the municipality's land area remained unclaimed: only 22 per cent of the land was reported in farms (IBGE 1970a). Almost all of the remaining public domain was on the poor soils of the terra firme interior. Nonetheless, with respect to available land resources, the peasant population had several alternatives to dependence on large landowners.

The size of large properties recorded by the 1970 census was moderate by Brazilian Amazonian standards. Only seventeen farms fell into the category of 1,000 or more hectares, and they averaged only 1,557.5 hectares (Table 5).[7] They were owned by the urban elite of Itacoatiara and residents of Manaus. Most used only a small fraction of their property for pasture, predominantly natural pasture in the varzea (Table 7). A further indication of the lack of large-scale agricultural enterprise is the fact that in 1970 the permanent labour force in the agricultural sector was almost entirely composed of farm owners or operators and their families. Other permanent labour totalled 107 individuals, or less than 2 per cent of the permanent labour force in the primary sector.

Thus the agricultural sector in 1970 consisted mainly of small peasant farmers and small livestock raisers who did not compete seriously for land and labour. Land was primarily appreciated and transacted for its use.

SOCIAL ORGANIZATION

In 1970 Itacoatiara's social organization was not complex. A small number of local urban-based families, several of Lebanese extraction, controlled the export-import trade, most of the credit and supplies for the

---

7. Some land claims established by extraregional speculators during the latter part of the 1960s may have escaped the 1970 census.

regatoes, rural traders and primary producers, as well as the municipal government. Thus most of the population directly or indirectly depended on these local entrepreneurs. They were also the only wealthy families, but their wealth was of a modest nature which in no way reflected the ostentatious consumption of the rubber period. The importance of some of these families dated from that period, in particular the Mamedes, Lebanese immigrants who had operated the trading house Irmãos Mamede since 1908 and the guaraná bottling plant since 1953 (Tables 2 and 3). Another prominent family of Lebanese origin were the Chiblys who owned Usina Cecy, the only rubber-processing plant. In 1970 these local families shared economic power with only two companies based outside the municipality—I.B. Sabba, a jute, extractive products and petroleum firm based in Manaus, and Brasiljuta of Rio de Janeiro. The remainder of the traditional local elite consisted of smaller urban store owners and a limited circle of liberal professionals as well as the occasional civil servant from Manaus who managed to stay on or acquire property in the area.

Most of this urban-based elite owned land in the surrounding countryside. The importance of its landholdings, however, was generally secondary to its urban pursuits.

The Associação Comercial was exclusive to the economic elite, which also met in the Masonic Lodge and the Lions Club. The Sindicato Rural, in contrast, was an 870-member organization (SUDAM 1970:34) composed of both large landowners and peasant owners, although it was dominated by the former. The socially mixed membership of the Sindicato Rural indicates the limited class consciousness, let alone class antagonism, in the rural sector. The diverse interests represented within it, together with the fact that most of the larger landowners had primarily urban-centred interests, made the Sindicato rather ineffectual in exerting effective pressure for rural development. Most of the elite pressure was expended on upgrading urban facilities.

The masses, meanwhile, lacked organizations to represent their interests. In the city, four labour unions existed, but in name only. The prevalence of seasonal employment, high rates of unemployment and underemployment, cyclical fluctuations of the local export economy, and the absence of a tradition of long-term urban employment were major obstacles to urban unionization. These factors would have been sufficient barriers to effective unionization even if the political climate had been more amenable.

In the countryside, conditions for community organization were equally unpromising. The river zone peasant led a solitary existence in spite of the fact that rural population densities in the Middle Amazon were higher than in other parts of the Brazilian Amazon. Isolation was only occasionally interrupted by some religious festival, a gathering in connection with the rare visit of the priest, or infrequent excursions to town. Reliance on the canoe for transport, the interruption of overland transportation during the flood season, and a tradition of isolated existence in conjunction with the extractive economy are responsible for the low level of communication and social organization in comparison with other peasant societies.

Given the dearth of social organization and the limited government initiatives with regard to organizing the population, a central leadership role fell to the Roman Catholic Church. The Canadian Scarborough Mission Society, which in 1965 took charge of the Prelacy of Itacoatiara, was short-staffed and had to concentrate its efforts in the city, where it maintained four churches, three social centres, a hospital, and a secondary school. Most of the river zone received only periodic visits by a priest. To compensate, the Prelacy followed the guidelines of the 1964 Plano Pastoral de Conjunto da Amazônia for the development of basic Christian communities (cebs) with particular emphasis on the rural areas. In doing so, the Prelacy was strongly influenced by the dynamic within the progressive Brazilian Church.

It began training rural catechists in 1966 and instituted a training centre (CENTREPI) for a variety of community leaders in 1968 (Mendonça Leite 1981:8). By the end of the 1960s, cebs were springing up throughout the countryside, often organized around a community-built structure that served as school, church, and meeting hall. Soon ceb activists used the emerging human networks for other forms of community organization to the extent that the terms "basic Christian community" and "community" became largely interchangeable in local usage. This foundation laid by the Church in the 1960s would support much of the community organization and development of the 1970s.

2. EXPANSION OF THE BRAZILIAN SYSTEM INTO ITACOATIARA

Since the late 1960s a range of new government entities and programs as well as new private enterprises have made their presence felt in Itacoatiara, while some of the established local actors have changed their activities. Generally, local change has been led by federal and state initiatives, with private enterprise responding to the new opportunities. Although some private sector response can be related to individual government services and incentives, it is difficult to single out specific cause-effect relationships. Private enterprise initiatives are best understood as reacting to and benefitting from a package of new public sector facilities and the climate of expectation of further improvements which accompanies it.

ZONA FRANCA AND ROAD NETWORK EXPANSION

The initial and most important modern development impetus for the Middle Amazon in general, and Itacoatiara in particular, was the creation of the Zona Franca de Manaus in 1967 (Decree-Law No. 288) under the direction of SUFRAMA, the federal Superintendency of the Manaus Free Trade Zone. The 10,000 square kilometre Zona Franca borders Itacoatiara to the West and includes the northwestern extremity of the municipality. It represents the federal commitment to the development and integration of the western and central Amazon. Thus it focused attention on, and created opportunities in, an area which otherwise would have been bypassed by the process of the contiguous expansion of the more accessible frontier on the southern and eastern fringes of Amazonia.

After the creation of the Zona Franca, Manaus, which had been the foremost city within the state of Amazonas since the rubber period, expanded at a rate faster than any state capital in Legal Amazonia except for Cuiabá. Its population swelled from 173,703 in 1960 to 312,160 in 1970 and reached 634,759 ten years later. Meanwhile the proportion of the state's population concentrated in Manaus jumped from 24 per cent in 1960 to 45 per cent in 1980 (Benchimol 1985).

The initial development of the Zona Franca has been appropriately characterized as that of an artificial enclave economy (Mahar 1976, 1979), based as it was on a booming trade in duty-free consumer goods and a host of new industries primarily engaged in the assembly of imported components. Initial centralization of new infrastructure and services, including the industrial park of Manaus and normal agglomeration economies, soon established a pattern of polarized growth in a region of underequipped secondary centres.

The increased importance of Manaus necessitated a program of accelerated road construction to link the city to its hinterland and to modern Brazil in the South. The state highway department (DER-AM) placed priority on connecting the state's two most important cities, Manaus and Itacoatiara, by linking penetration roads which had been gradually extended earlier from the two centres. A precarious dirt road connection, which was initially shunned by bus companies, had been opened in 1965. Its trajectory followed well-drained interfluves to minimize construction and maintenance problems and thus bypassed the previously settled riverine zone. Under favourable circumstances *colectivos* (taxis) could complete the trip between the cities in approximately twelve hours. By 1979 parts of the trajectory had been straightened and shortened and the total distance of 270 kilometres was paved, providing a reliable all-season connection. It is now covered in approximately four and one-half hours by scheduled bus service five times a day in each direction.

By the end of 1973, Manaus was connected to the transportation network of South-Central Brazil and to the Transamazônica by a paved federal highway to Porto Velho (BR 319). In 1976 the federal highway BR 174 established a dirt road connection from Manaus to Boa Vista and Venezuela.

The spatial and functional implications for Itacoatiara of this new road network are threefold: Itacoatiara was suddenly opened to new markets and external influences; the municipality's terra firme interior, henceforth referred to as the road zone, gained accessibility at the expense of the river zone; and lands in the western half of the municipality (that is, West of 59°W) came under the administration of INCRA according to Decree-Law 1164 of 1971, which specifies that throughout Amazonia the area within 100 kilometres of federal roads—in this case BR 319 and BR 174—falls under federal jurisdiction.

The spectacular growth of the Zona Franca and the concurrent expansion of the road network into the Middle Amazon have triggered a series of unprecedented changes in Itacoatiara. In general terms, these are a reflection of the broader process of modernization which engulfed the Brazilian Amazon during the 1970s and which, increasingly, reaches more remote localities like Itacoatiara. Yet the local process of change is given particular character by the fact that it largely involves a long-established caboclo population in a particular physical context which juxtaposes river zone and terra firme interior, and by its proximity to a booming urban centre and continuing relative remoteness from the core areas of the country.

The simple and stable set of actors which prevailed in the early 1960s has been replaced by a far more complex system of actors and programs that impinge on the municipality's development. These involve both governmental agencies and private enterprise originating outside the municipality, as well as traditional actors within the municipality who are changing their roles and new actors emerging on the local stage. Their characteristics, roles, and interrelationships will be set out in this chapter before the major processes of change are discussed in Chapter 4.

SUFRAMA

The establishment of the Zona Franca under the management of SUFRAMA had both detrimental and beneficial impacts on the development of Itacoatiara. The detrimental effects are more immediate and more visible. As the relative advantage of Manaus over surrounding centres in all areas of urban services and opportunities increased sharply, Itacoatiara suffered from outmigration that included an important component of educated and skilled labour. Furthermore, the expansion of the municipality's commerce, particularly in consumer durables, was severely affected by competition from duty-free imports available in Manaus because customs controls at the boundaries of the Zona Franca were ineffective. Only the fact that much of Itacoatiara's population was debt dependent on local commercial establishments, and thus a captive market, prevented a more traumatic impact on local commerce.

Apart from these major adjustments, the impact of SUFRAMA on the municipality has been generally positive in economic terms. Manaus has grown into a large market for primary products, mainly for internal consumption, which producers in Itacoatiara have thus far failed to exploit adequately. As well, the services and inputs available in the Zona Franca facilitate the installation and functioning of modern enterprise in the hinterland.

An important step toward decentralization of development beyond the boundaries of the Zona Franca was the introduction of selected SUFRAMA incentives to the remainder of western Amazonia in 1968. In that year, certain development essentials, including transport and agricultural equipment, construction materials, foodstuffs, and drugs were freed from import duty (Decree-Law No. 356). Access to these incentives is facilitated by a SUFRAMA office in Itacoatiara, which in 1981 boasted a list of fifty-seven registered beneficiaries.

Furthermore, SUFRAMA has created an agricultural district encompassing the northwestern fringe of the municipality in which medium-sized (500 to 3,000 hectares) and small rural enterprises receive duty-free inputs and a range of other support services in order to generate raw materials for processing and consumption in the Zona Franca.

AMAZONAS STATE DECENTRALIZATION MEASURES

In the 1970s, the government of the state of Amazonas, like SUFRAMA, manifested an increasing interest in decentralizing economic development. A hierarchy of growth and service centres was conceived to guide the strengthening of infrastructure and services in smaller centres (for example, SEPLAN 1976, SEPLAN/CODEAMA 1980). In this plan, Itacoatiara figures just below Manaus as one of five subregional centres. Though no concerted program of action has yet materialized, a number of individual measures have significantly improved the city's prospect for growth. Notable among these are the installation of a floating dock capable of handling ocean-going ships, major expansion of the urban power supply, and construction of a hospital.

In addition, in 1979 a value-added tax (ICM) remission scheme came into effect to the benefit of industrial and agricultural enterprises located outside the Zona Franca which use local raw materials or which are involved in the production of a range of priority goods (State Law No. 1370). Local enterprises can access these benefits by registering with the Itacoatiara office of the State of Amazonas Department of Revenue.

SUDAM INCENTIVES

Fiscal incentives under the auspices of SUDAM, applicable in Itacoatiara as elsewhere in Legal Amazonia, have made a limited contribution to local development. Because they are, in practice, confined to larger firms and access requires a high level of sophistication, particularly in view of the absence of a local office to provide assistance, only a small number of enterprises have made use of the generous subsidies available from this source.

In 1965 (that is, before the creation of SUDAM in 1967), Itacoatiara Industrial, a Manaus-controlled sawmill which had operated in the city since 1952, had availed itself of incentives provided by SPVEA (Superintendência do Plano de Valorização Econômica da Amazônia), the predecessor of SUDAM. In 1975 and 1976 two locally owned lumber-processing enterprises followed suit by applying to SUDAM. Both involved the Mamoud family: Serraria Progresso, which had existed since 1971, and Compensados Itacoatiara, established in 1975.

In the agricultural sector, Itacoatiara has few enterprises sufficiently large and sophisticated to qualify for SUDAM-financed projects. None of the locally owned, traditionally managed enterprises which dominate in the eastern half of the municipality have benefitted. In the western half, which is under INCRA jurisdiction, the official maximum property size limit of 3,000 hectares discouraged the entry of large firms. Only one enterprise in the western half used SUDAM incentives, the externally owned Fazendas Unidas, which managed to assemble and legalize a 24,000-hectare unit. Furthermore, after gaining clout by establishing a partnership with CAPEMI, the military pension fund, it subsequently succeeded in obtaining Pro-Alcool incentives.

The success rate of these enterprises (Itacoatiara Industrial, Serraria Progresso, Compensados Itacoatiara, and Fazendas Unidas), all of which obtained incentive funds far exceeding their own capital investments, is disappointing. It reflects the considerable difficulties faced by modern enterprises in a frontier environment and the speculative attitude engendered by relatively low financial risk. Fazendas Unidas faced the added obstacle of low soil fertility.

By 1981 only two of the SUDAM beneficiaries—Compensados Itacoatiara and Serraria Progresso—functioned normally, the latter having been sold to a Paraná-based company after expanding with SUDAM financing. Itacoatiara Industrial was no longer operational. Fazendas Unidas had almost completely abandoned its initial project of livestock raising, lumber extraction, and manioc production, and had shifted to sugar-cane-based alcohol production under the auspices of Pro-Alcool.

AGRICULTURAL CREDIT

The previously described fiscal incentives are the domain of larger enterprise. The reform of locally available bank credit in conjunction with federal programs favouring crop agriculture and small producers which took place during the 1970s is tantamount to a fiscal incentives scheme for the mass of the rural population. Banking services had existed in Itacoatiara since the early 1950s. The three banks in operation during the 1970s expanded their services somewhat, yet failed to keep pace with local requirements. In 1981, this relatively significant centre in Amazonia's primary export economy still lacked facilities for foreign exchange transactions. The redirection of agricultural credit, however, was well ahead of the capacity of the local population to utilize it effectively.

In the early 1970s, credit was still mainly channelled to larger clients involved in commerce, industry, and livestock raising. From 1978 to 1980, however, when the volume of credit increased substantially before starting to shrink in 1981, a drastic change in the allocation of credit took place. It favoured peasant producers, small acreage projects, and the principal peasant products—jute and food crops. Also, crop credit was distinguished from other lines of credit by being highly subsidized. The explosive growth of crop credit allocated to peasant producers is illustrated by statistics from the Banco do Brasil, the main purveyor of credit in Itacoatiara. Its crop loans increased from 1,307 in 1978 to 2,169 in 1979 and to 7,181 in 1980 (unpublished data).

It is evident that sustained application of subsidized credit at this scale could have fundamentally altered local socio-economic structures. It could have consolidated the local economy on a broad base of primary producers with multiplier effects deriving from increased raw material production and consumer demand. Concurrently the peasantry could have been liberated from its debt dependence on traditional intermediaries, thus setting in motion a fundamental modernization and democratization process. These ramifications will be examined in Chapter 3.

RURAL SERVICES

The reorientation of credit toward increased support of peasant farmers has been accompanied by major improvements in other rural support services, particularly with regard to production inputs, extension work, and land tenure regularization, which by and large have been increasingly supportive of small producers.

In 1976 CODEAGRO (Companhia de Desenvolvimento Agropecuário do Amazonas), a mixed company with the State of Amazonas and SUFRAMA as major shareholders, opened an outlet in Itacoatiara which supplies the full range of agricultural inputs in local demand and operates a nursery for rubber seedlings.

In the area of rural extension, EMATER, which replaced ACAR in 1977, is the dominant agency. In 1981, it had a local staff of seventeen. The fields of specialization to which its eleven technicians were assigned in 1981 are indicative of EMATER's priorities.[8]

In 1979–80, except for servicing a small number of medium and larger livestock raisers, EMATER focused most of its attention on existing communities. In 1981 it serviced only those peasant producers who were actively involved in organized communities, which generally meant that they were members of basic Christian communities. This approach reflects an attempt to maximize the impact of limited personnel as well as a policy to foster the formation of communities.

EMATER's selectivity in favour of organized communities is extremely important because this agency practically determines the allocation of credit. The banks have too few personnel to supervise more than a small number of agricultural loans, and they normally concentrate on larger clients. Thus EMATER was entrusted with the bulk of the applications for crop loans, the subsequent monitoring of credit in the agricultural sector, and the accompanying agricultural extension service.

EMATER's central role in the allocation and monitoring of credit excludes only jute and cacao. In 1981 the agency relinquished its involvement in the supervision of jute credit for two reasons. First, it recognized that it had little pertinent expertise to offer jute farmers whose well-established traditional practices required little change. Second, EMATER's limited manpower and its single boat precluded effective supervision of dispersed jute farmers in the extensive river zone of the municipality, especially given the seasonal vagaries of local accessibility. This retreat from extension work with jute farmers, however, has not affected EMATER's work in building communities in the river zone, carried out through tele-extension and periodic seminars with groups of community members in a central location.

Extension work and credit supervision relating to the small number of cacao projects which had been initiated during the late 1970s were shifted from EMATER to CEPLAC in 1980 when the latter opened an Itacoatiara office with one agronomist and a technician. Though the installation of the CEPLAC office appeared to indicate the government's intention to foster the expansion of the cacao acreage in the municipality, in 1980-1981

---

8. Number and specialty of EMATER technicians at the Itacoatiara Agency in 1981: 4, community development; 1, social development; 1 cooperativism; 1, tele-extension; 2, rubber; 1, fishing; 1, cattle. Total: 11.

CEPLAC managed to arrange bank financing for only six small projects out of forty-two applications for funding which it helped to prepare.

The last locally established agency involved in the supervision of rural resource use is IBDF (Instituto Brasileiro de Desenvolvimento Florestal). With seven employees and one boat, the IBDF office is unable to fulfill its mandate of monitoring forest use in a huge area encompassing several neighbouring municipalities. It thus confines its attention to lumber sold by the processing plants in the city.

Land tenure was previously a wholly neglected concern, but major steps were taken during the 1970s in recognition of the rapidly changing de facto tenure and the demand for formalization of tenure in a modernizing agricultural economy. At the end of the 1970s, both INCRA and ITERAM, which replaced the ineffectual SEPROR in 1979, started a complete review and provisional cartography of existing tenure in their respective jurisdictions. In ITERAM's case, this included the twenty-kilometre radius around the city where land tenure normally falls under municipal jurisdiction, since the municipal government failed to assume its responsibility. This process was largely completed in 1981, though results were not available for public inspection.

Meanwhile, the issuing of legal titles proceeded slowly throughout the 1970s and was stalled altogether during the tenure-review process, ostensibly because of the confused state of historical land claims. The majority of large land claims had not yet been converted to definitive titles by 1981. Only in the corridor immediately adjacent to the highway within the area of INCRA jurisdiction and in a few communities of the road hinterland within ITERAM jurisdiction were titles awarded, generally upon concerted pressure from organized peasant communities and during election periods when the federal and state governments were seeking electoral support. The process is encumbered by the fact that title requests are processed in Manaus. The INCRA officer in Itacoatiara is confined to the maintenance of the cadaster, based on unverified self-declarations of property owners for land tax purposes. ITERAM's local three-person staff only accumulates the data base upon which decisions are made in the Manaus head office.

PRIVATE ENTERPRISE

The expansion of infrastructure and services since the first dirt road was linked to the exterior in 1967 has led to a substantial increase in the number of large private enterprises. Extra-regional entrepreneurs moved into the lumber industry and the agricultural sector, while local entrepreneurs diversified their areas of activity. Though the factors determining location and expansion of individual enterprises vary, it is apparent that new infrastructure, services, and incentives played an important role in most cases (Table 8).

TABLE 8   Location Determinants, Incentive Use, and Bank Financing of Selected Major Industrial and Agricultural Enterprises Established or Purchased since 1970

Name (Year of foundation/ acquisition; main product)	Ownership L = local E = external	Location Determinants	Incentives Used	Banks Used
Serraria União (1974; lumber)	L	local owner	none	BEA BNDES
Indústria Trevo (1979; lumber)	E	infrastructure, proximity of Manaus, strategic location	none	BEA
Atlantic Veneer (1976; plywood, veneer)	E	strategic location	SUDAM (IR), SUFRAMA, ICM, municipal	none
Gethal (1978; lumber)	E	strategic location, proximity of Manaus, fiscal incentives	SUDAM (IR, IPI), ICM	none
Correia Indústria e Comercio (1976; jute)	L	local resources	SUDAM (IPI), ICM	BEA BASA
Frigorífico Rio Mar (1973; ice)	L	local owner, local demand	none	BB
Indústria Gelopesca (1975; ice)	L	local owner, local demand	none	BEA
Fazenda W.M. (1975; cattle)	E	fiscal incentives, cheap land	cheap state land	BASA
Fazenda São Joaquim (1974; cattle)	E	fiscal incentives, cheap land	cheap state land	BASA
Agropecuária Bom Jesus (1976; cattle)	E	fiscal incentives, cheap land	none	BASA
Fazenda Sta. Rita (1972; cattle)	L	local owner	none	none

Source: Elite Survey 1981.

The lumber industry is now dominated by three new firms from Southern Brazil. These include Atlantic Veneer (based in Vitoria, Espiritu Santo), which produces sawn lumber, veneer and plywood, and ships logs to its plant in Vitoria, as well as the saw mills of Gethal (based in Porto Alegre, Rio Grande do Sul), and Indústria Trevo da Amazônia (based in Curitiba, Paraná), the latter having absorbed the previously locally owned Serraria Progresso. With a combined permanent labour force of approximately 750, these three enterprises in 1980 accounted for over 80 per cent of lumber industry employment, 12 per cent of the secondary-tertiary sector employment, and more than 6 per cent of the municipality's total active labour force (Survey, IBGE 1980c).

The determinant for these lumber enterprises is Itacoatiara's strategic location in relation to the vast fluvial hinterland of western Amazonia and the existence of a large lagoon a short distance upriver from the city which permits year-round log storage. Raw material is assured, mainly by a network of intermediaries in upriver locations well removed from the municipality. Thus road access to local timber resources is of minor importance to the industries, although highly significant for roadside landowners.

The increasing availability of modern services in Manaus has been crucial to all the lumber enterprises, although their administrative personnel from the South tend to ridicule Manaus facilities and many inputs are supplied directly from the head offices. Improvements to Itacoatiara's power supply and port facilities were instrumental in the successful installation of these enterprises. In contrast, fiscal incentives were not instrumental during installation but assumed a role in the long-term viability of the firms and in the context of subsequent expansion plans.

The new enterprises not only benefitted from, but, by playing a leading lobbying role, contributed to the improvement of infrastructure and services. Atlantic Veneer, for example, used its leverage as the biggest firm and Itacoatiara's main hope for employment generation to pressure the municipal and state governments into expanding the power supply. In 1981 it led the lobby for the improvement of bank services to permit international transactions.

While new southern enterprises clearly dominate the industrial sector and have made important contributions to the modernization of the local economy and to employment generation, the same cannot be said for southern enterprise in the agricultural sector. Since the initial days of road construction, the attention of southern enterprises, though rarely of big companies, has been attracted to this area which promised speculative gains because of the rapid growth of Manaus, the priority given by the state to road paving, and access to the lumber industries of Itacoatiara. Thus it was not surprising that Paulistas and a few other entrepreneurs acquired the bulk of the previously unsettled road hinterland except in the vicinity of Itacoatiara city, that is, the area up to the first Urubu River crossing (Figure 2), where local landholders were already established. In the western, INCRA-administered part of the municipality, most of the land was claimed in 3,000-

hectare units, Fazendas Unidas being the major exception. Meanwhile, the already-settled river zone was barely affected.

For a number of reasons, few of the new landowners undertook major projects. Control of the land was essentially speculative. The area was still quite remote compared to the dynamic frontiers farther south. The soils were exceptionally poor. The locally available caboclo labour was neither sufficiently reliable nor sufficiently deprived of access to land to represent an ideal workforce. Token land clearing and ranching to fend off squatters, or no development at all, were common.

The dramatic expansion of externally based private enterprise in the lumber industry and in the rural sector has not significantly impinged on the interests of the local economic elite. The city water supply, power-generating capacity, port facilities, and potential industrial sites are sufficient to permit additional entries into the lumber industry and expansion of other economic activities. In the countryside, competition for land with the local elite was minimized because extra-regional entrepreneurs generally avoided the immediate road hinterland of the city.

Only one out-of-state enterprise has entered into direct competition with local firms while establishing itself as a locally based firm. This is the family firm of Alvaro Correia. It acquired a major establishment that processes and exports jute, Brazil nuts, and cacao; opened a supermarket; rented a locally owned sawmill (Tables 9 and 10); and purchased a *fazenda* (large farm) in the immediate hinterland of the city.

The established local elite has expanded and diversified its economic activities while continuing to control the municipal government. As a case in point, the city's Lebanese families have reinforced their prominent position by opening a plywood factory, an ice plant which primarily services the expanding commercial fishery, and a brick factory. They also acquired a second ice plant which had been established by a Japanese entrepreneur from Manaus, and the city's petroleum products terminal which had been operated by the Manaus-based Sabba Company (Table 9).

A larger number of local entrepreneurs were involved in the expansion of the urban tertiary sector. This expansion was facilitated by increased consumer demand and improved availability of supplies via Manaus. Several larger stores, service and repair establishments, restaurants, and two hotels were added. Most of the numerical increase of tertiary-sector establishments from 255 in 1970 (IBGE 1970c, 1970d) to 842 in 1980 (IBGE 1980d, 1980e), however, was due to a proliferation of the informal sector.

Finally, the urban elite involved itself increasingly in the rural sector, particularly in the immediate terra firme hinterland of the city, or up to the first Urubu River crossing. This process was encouraged by improved market access, by the prospect of rising land values in the wake of road paving and feeder road construction, and by the increased availability of agricultural credit. It involved expansion of previously held property as well as first-time acquisition of land and produced a higher proportion of pasture development than prevails in the areas controlled by extra-regional entrepreneurs. Properties under the control of the local elite range from a few hundred to 3,000 hectares. The majority of these can be monitored by their urban owners and utilize surplus urban labour on a day-by-day basis because they are located within easy driving distance of the city.

The numerical increase and diversification of interests among Itacoatiara's private enterprise elite during the 1970s has not been accompanied by a parallel development of private sector institutions which can coherently represent class interests. The long-established Associação Commercial and the Sindicato Rural Patronal languished because of poor leadership and lackluster support from their memberships. Conflicts within the Sindicato eventually led to the creation of the Associação dos Criadores, which mainly represents *fazendeiros* (large landowners). Major obstacles to organization among the power holders included the lack of integration between external and local elites because of their divergent mentalities and interests, the prevalence of absentee ownership among external owners, increased heterogeneity of the municipality's economic enterprises, and the political and personal conflicts among the local elite which are particularly apparent at election time. A symptom of this lack of organization among the elite is the fact that Itacoatiara has not even managed to sustain a newspaper.

THE CHURCH

The expanding elite failed to develop new institutions to represent its class interests, but major changes took place in the 1970s with regard to institutions representing popular interests. Though the emerging popular institutions have encountered numerous problems and setbacks, their achievements are impressive in view of the atomization and traditionalism of caboclo society which still prevailed in the 1960s. As the only existing institution with firm roots among the masses, the Roman Catholic Church has played the central role in this organization process. It has done so through its own program of community formation, by becoming the most audible voice of popular concerns, and by providing support for other popular institutions. The influence of the Church was doubtless enhanced by its access to financial and human resources, both foreign and national.

In 1965 the Prelacy of Itacoatiara, which encompasses a total of five municipalities, was entrusted to the relatively progressive Scarborough Mission Society of Canada. These priests and nuns soon began to follow wholeheartedly the policy changes of the increasingly socially committed Church in Brazil. When conflicts between the economic elite and the masses multiplied in the 1970s, the Prelacy naturally came out on the side of the poor. This alliance alienated many of the local elite, sparked attacks by the municipal government, and even provoked threatening appearances by the federal police.

As elsewhere in Brazil, probably the most important innovation of the Church was the creation of basic Christian communities (cebs), a democratization process following the guidelines of liberation theology, in

TABLE 9   *Industrial Establishments with Five or More Workers, 1970 and 1981*

Name (Year of foundation)	Ownership in 1981 L = local[a] E = external	Main products	Operating in		Labour force in 1981
			1970	1981	
Brasiljuta (1962)	E	jute, cacao	X	X	105
I.B. Sabba (1955)	E	jute, Brazil nuts, sorva, rosewood	X	X	76
Cooperativa Mista (1968)	L	jute, various crops	X	X	136
Correia Indústria e Comercio (1954) (sold 1976) (Correia)	L	jute, Brazil nuts, cacao	X	X	80
Itacoatiara Industrial (1952)	E	lumber	X	—	—
Serraria Boa Vista (1979) (Correia)	L	lumber	—	X	49
Compensados Itacoatiara (1975) (Mamoud)	L	plywood, veneer	—	X	84
Serraria Uniao (1974) (Matos)	L	lumber	—	X	53
Indústria Trevo (formerly Serraria Progresso) (1971) (sold 1979)	E	lumber	—	X	84
Atlantic Veneer (1976)	E	plywood, veneer	—	X	510
Gethal (1978)	E	lumber	—	X	127

Usina Cecy (1955) (Chibly)	L	rubber	X	X	60
Olaria Sta Maria (1976) (Chibly)	L	bricks	—	X	25
Olaria Sto António (1955) (sold 1980)	L	bricks	X	X	11
Olaria Santo Céu (1978)	?	brick, tile	—	X	18
Guaraná Rio Negro (1953) (Mamede)	L	soft drinks	X	X	6
Frigorífico Rio Mar (1973) (Lekakis)	L	ice	—	X	22
Indústria Gelopesca (1975) (Chibly)	L	ice	—	X	19
Fazendas Unidas (1975)	E	alcohol	—	X	?
Matadouro Municipal (1920)	L	meat	X	X	12

Source: Elite Survey, CEAG-AM n.d.
a For locally owned family firms, the surname of the principal current owner appears in parentheses.

TABLE 10   *Commercial Establishments with Five or More Workers, 1970 and 1981*

Name (Year of foundation)	Ownership L = local[a] E = external	Main Products	Operating in 1970	Operating in 1981	Labour force in 1981
Irmãos Mamede (1908) (Mamede)	L	general merchandise	X	X	11
Ipenor Menezes (1963) (Menezes)	L	general merchandise	X	X	14
Chibly Cia Terminal de Petroleo (?) (Chibly)	L	petroleum products	X	X	20
CODEAGRO (1976)	E	agricultural inputs	—	X	16
A.S. Cardoso Cia (1974) (Cardoso)	L	textiles, consumer durables	—	X	6
Supermercado Na Sra de Fatima (1976) (Correia)	L	food products	—	X	9

Source: Elite Survey.

[a]For locally owned family firms, the surname of the principal current owner appears in parentheses.

which the laity is given a key role and encouragement to relate the gospel to local socio-economic reality. Given the small number of priests in Itacoatiara and their inability to attend regularly to the dispersed rural population, ceb formation was particularly urgent in the rural areas.

After the creation of a training centre for community leaders (CENTREPI) in 1968, the numerical growth of cebs accelerated, reaching sixty-eight communities in 1972. The work of progressive priests lent by the sister Archdiocese of São Paulo from 1974 onward contributed greatly to a further expansion to 159 cebs in 1980. Of these, ninety-one were located in the municipality of Itacoatiara: sixty-four in the river zone, eighteen in the road zone, and only nine in the city where over half of the municipality's population was concentrated (Mendonça Leite 1981:9; Bruneau 1986:116).

This disproportionate distribution reflects both the priority given to the river zone, where the church has maintained an involvement of long standing with the traditional, relatively stable population, and the greater organizational difficulties in the road zone with its more heterogeneous population and higher turnover rates. Limited attention was given to ceb formation in the city, where four churches and two social centres provided alternatives and where other urban services competed for the population's attention.

Rural cebs are generally organized around a primary school and chapel, which often use the same building. In several cases they have started to attract a small cluster of primary and secondary residences. As the only community organizations of any significance in the countryside, cebs have become the predominant framework for the rural work of other popular organizations as well as the banks, such state agencies as EMATER and ITERAM, and the municipal government. Equally significant of the influence of the Church on emerging popular institutions is the fact that most of their leadership is drawn from the approximately 1,000 community leaders who had attended CENTREPI courses by 1980. Thus, though the Church has sought to refrain from direct involvement in the affairs of other popular institutions except during their formative stages, several links, key individuals, and commonality of purpose have remained. It is doubtful whether other popular institutions would have managed to establish themselves and survive without the helping hand of the Church.

THE COOPERATIVA MISTA AGROPECUÁRIA DE ITACOATIARA (CMAI)

At least since the mid-1970s, the Church had been concerned with the control exerted by the local commercial elite over caboclo producers. This led it to promote the Cooperativa Mista Agropecuária (CMAI), which was built in 1968 on the foundations of a church-managed savings and consumer cooperative. Top management was provided by ACAR and its successor EMATER, with the remainder of its personnel drawn from the local population. Initial material assistance was furnished by the Church.

CMAI's principal objective has been to reduce the control of the major export establishments and of the traders in the interior which supply them by providing a marketing alternative managed by the peasant producers. In response to the diversity of peasant production, CMAI handles a greater range of products (including farinha, rice, beans, maize and guaraná) than its three major competitors. Like them, however, its main product is jute, and the majority of CMAI membership is composed of river zone jute producers.

During its initial decade of existence, CMAI's performance fluctuated and was generally unimpressive. Its fortunes improved substantially after it moved from a disadvantageous site to the riverfront in 1978, at approximately the same time that the credit-inspired agricultural production boom began.[9] In 1980 CMAI started to serve as an intermediary for the Banco do Brasil, administering production credit for 105 members. In the same year, BB financed membership shares for 262 members. It was not surprising that membership figures surged in 1980 from 212 to 539 (CMAI 1980), with a further increase to 635 in 1981 (Elite Survey).

This membership surge, which hardly reflects a breakthrough in cooperativist spirit among the peasantry, has not yet fundamentally altered the agricultural products market. Rather than making progress toward the eventual displacement of its three main private competitors, one of which entered the field four years after the cooperative was founded, CMAI has carved out only a modest share of a growing market. In 1981, cooperative membership, which includes many peasants from neighbouring municipalities, still corresponded to only 35 per cent of Itacoatiara's jute growers—CMAI's main clientele—or 19 per cent of the municipality's farm operators. Only 147 producers (27 per cent of the year-end membership) delivered jute to CMAI in 1980 (CMAI 1980). These figures indicate that a large proportion of the membership continues to deal with CMAI's main competitors and the network of traders supplying them.

CMAI's limited control of peasant production is partly attributable to the cooperative's inadequate transport facilities, the absence of warehouses in the hinterland precluding effective servicing of the membership, and delayed payment for crops received. Furthermore, the cooperative has come increasingly under the control of larger producers with their own means of transportation or ability to contract transport, some of whom also function as traders. This development has only reinforced the tendency of many caboclos to look upon the cooperative as just another patrão.

OBRAS SOCIAIS CERÁMICA E SERRARIA LTDA. (SERRARIA UNIÃO)

A second church-inspired experiment in cooperativism which has increasingly departed from its original objectives, is Obras Sociais

---

9. CMAI jute purchases: 1976, 100 tons; 1977, 200 tons; 1978, 475 tons; 1979, 1,010 tons; 1980, 1,183 tons. (CMAI 1980).

Cerámica e Serraria Ltda., popularly known as Serraria União. It emerged in the early 1970s from a neighbourhood savings club under the leadership of a priest who managed to obtain funding from the Canadian Catholic Organization for Development and Peace. Its objective was to produce cheap materials for home construction because brick and tile produced in existing *olarias* (brickyards) were too expensive and the lumber industries essentially served the export market.

Serraria União started operations in a rented olaria but eventually moved to a Church-supplied site on the riverbank. Here it constructed a sawmill and redirected its production to construction lumber under the able management of a member who had previously acquired experience as an employee of the local lumber industries. The founding priest was then able to withdraw from the smoothly functioning operation. When the first generation of members had succeeded in constructing their homes, however, interest in the cooperative waned. The manager's family was able to acquire the majority of shares, effectively turning the sawmill into a family enterprise which, in 1981, employed a labour force of fifty. Though Serraria União now directs half of its growing production to the export market, it distinguishes itself from the other lumber industries by maintaining a strong and personalized relationship with the local and regional market and flexible, often concessionary, dealings with its lower-class clientele.

THE SINDICATO DOS TRABALHADORES RURAIS (STR)

Of greater importance than the cooperative movement is the Sindicato dos Trabalhadores Rurais (STR), a union of small farmers rather than of landless labourers, since STR has found it too difficult to organize the latter. The Itacoatiara STR was founded in 1972 by the Confederação Nacional dos Trabalhadores Rurais (CONTAG) shortly after the latter established a regional federation in Manaus. It is supervised by the Ministry of Labour, which provides the bulk of STR's funding by allocating 60 per cent of the local rural property tax exclusively for purposes of legal assistance and education and which enforces abstention from political activity. In spite of this government leverage, STR has by and large maintained an independent stance, assisted by Ministry representatives in Manaus and Itacoatiara who have supported STR's objectives.

The Church furnished CENTREPI for union meetings until STR acquired its own premises in 1973. Several priests have consistently encouraged unionization in the cebs where most of STR's organizing has taken place. Most of the cebs now have a *delegado sindical* (union representative) who frequently rivals the ceb leader in importance.

Starting with an initial membership of approximately 500, STR's growth has been irregular. Bad administration and internal conflict caused it to falter in 1975–1976, but it reached a registered, albeit not necessarily paid-up, membership in excess of 3,000 by 1981 because of its success in attracting peasant members from the heterogeneous Sindicato Rural Patronal.

Throughout its history, STR's main objective has been to consolidate land tenure for small holders in the face of increasing competition for land. Its main achievement has been the organization and eventual titling of five small farmer colonies for families displaced by land conflicts and a series of three extraordinary floods which ravaged the varzea during the 1970s. All of these colonies are located on terra firme, three in the immediate road hinterland of the city, the others on terra firme pockets south of the Amazon. STR has also experienced some success in organizing active resistance and legal assistance for groups of squatters threatened by eviction. In contrast, the union's strategy to deprive large landholders of labour by encouraging the landless to seek their own holdings on yet-unoccupied public domain proved largely unsuccessful. In 1981 a new issue arose when a large number of peasants faced credit-repayment problems because of overextension, environmental difficulties, and low jute prices. STR organized mass demonstrations and succeeded in convincing the banks to adopt more lenient repayment terms.

Despite these achievements, the process of consciousness raising among the caboclos has proved disappointingly slow. Many caboclos regard the union as a patrão providing protection in time of need, and membership has correspondingly risen only in times of hardship, causing the union to experience continuous financial instability. For example, only a third of the membership paid their dues in 1981. Despite internal bickering which resembled that prevailing among the municipality's elite, STR was clearly perceived by the peasantry as a powerful body representing its interest.

Lack of innovation among the caboclos continuously frustrates the STR leadership. It inhibits their effective occupation of the public domain, and gives rise to quick sales of land and petty conflicts between neighbours. These disappointments have led STR to abandon plans for further colonies in the hope that the caboclos' growing awareness of the increasing lack of land around them will eventually encourage spontaneous colony formation.

COALITIONS AND CONFLICTS

The preceding review of major actors that have emerged or redefined themselves in the 1970s reflects the mixture of forces which has replaced the relatively simple relationship between a small local economic and political elite and an unorganized mass of caboclos. Growing friction between the nascent economic and political elite and popular movements has replaced the previously tranquil patron-client system.

The main antagonists are, on one side, the municipal government and the larger landowners of local origin, and, on the other, the Church and the Sindicato dos Trabalhadores Rurais. Antagonism tends to flare up around specific issues—primarily rural land conflicts and urban squatter and public service problems—but is also visible in a continuing, vituperative campaign between the municipal government and sectors of the Church. The fundamental issue is control over the caboclo population, with the municipal government increasingly attempting to absorb and co-opt the communities created by the Church and the STR. Whereas the Church sees in the communities the basis for a new, more participatory and democratic Church, the municipal government sees a power base for electoral purposes. Limited class cohesion of the caboclo population enhances the roles of these two actors as the local population of caboclos on its own has never created associations or organizations for promoting its interests.

The situation in which these primary actors find themselves is complex. The local elite is marginal in comparison with the economic power of the firms with their head offices in the South of Brazil, and there is evidence that their interests may diverge on specific issues. The political power of the local elite is also slight in comparison to the power of Amazonas state. There have been recent tensions between the mayor and the state deputy, who are members of different parties. There are also political splits within the local elite. Nor has the local elite formed enduring organizations to promote its own interests. Its relative marginality and political diversity lead it to seek support from the communities.

The fact that the Catholic Church, a transnational institution, is at the centre of organizing the caboclos indicates the low level of class cohesion and organizational development among the local population. Further, because of a tradition of patron-client relations, the increasing economic opportunities of Itacoatiara, and the now easily accessible Manaus, there is little pressure to change attitudes, particularly as there is no shortage of land. The organizational innovations of the Church, which sought to help the caboclos defend their interests, played a role for a time and then changed. The CMAI lost whatever identification it had with the caboclos; the Serraria Uniao became a private firm; and the STR went through hard times in the early 1980s when the key elements of its leadership became more active in politics than union activities—and in different political parties at that. The Church continues to provide the inspiration and the resources for popular organizations, but so far none of these initiatives has found an enduring basis. Further, it must be emphasized that the Church is working with largely marginal elements—the caboclos in the river zone who are continuously moving out. The Church has tended to neglect the peasants in the road areas and has very little contact with, or support from, the middle class in the city.

State and federal institutions have generally remained uninvolved in the conflicts between the municipal elite and the popular organizations, except for the state military police (and, on one occasion, the federal investigative police), which have sided with the municipal elite. Some public institutions are clearly biased in favour of one side or the other. SUDAM, SUFRAMA, BASA, and the State of Amazonas Department of Revenue, which handles state incentives, are associated with the elite because only larger enterprises can use their programs. EMATER, on the other hand, is strongly identified with the small producers and maintains close links with STR and

CMAI. Such other institutions as INCRA, ITERAM, BB and BEA cater to both in reasonably evenhanded fashion, though the local representatives of land agencies have been supportive of STR and cautiously critical of the land-concentration process. The agricultural credit programs (curtailed since 1981) of the banks and BB's support of CMAI were implicitly intended to weaken the control of the traditional commercial elite. The programs did not continue long enough, nor were they sufficiently coordinated to break this control. However, in comparison with some other parts of the Amazon, the popular organizations, weak as they may be, operate within a relatively supportive public institutional framework and enjoy the support of the Church. The local elite is not cohesive and cannot rely on the support of the external economic actors, the state government, or the bureaucracy. Given this situation, the caboclos should have some reasonable chance for improved conditions. Whether this will happen depends on factors to be discussed in Chapter 3.

3. PROCESSES OF STRUCTURAL CHANGE

The processes of structural change engendered by the arrival of modern Brazil with its new actors and programs and the growth of the traditional elite will be primarily examined with regard to their relevance to the mass of the local population.

SPATIAL REORGANIZATION AND MIGRATION

In general terms, the implicit development strategy which was applied to Itacoatiara was urban and road centred, a local replica of the emphasis prevailing throughout the Brazilian Amazon. It produced a significant shift in the relative advantage of the major areas of the municipality. Virtually all new physical infrastructure, with the exception of roads, was concentrated in the city. In addition to a spatially selective road network, the rural areas gained only a system of primary schools and *minipostos* (small health centres). These were in large part constructed with the assistance of local communities.

The neglect of rural infrastructure was doubtless partly due to the dispersal, low density, and limited productivity of the rural population, which did not justify major physical infrastructure investments. Where higher rural densities existed, primarily in better-endowed pockets of the river zone, the implementation of modern infrastructure faced particular difficulties due to flooding and poor drainage, erosion, and deposition processes in the varzea and discontinuous terrain.

Within the rural areas, selective government intervention shifted the relative advantage to the road zone, in spite of the superior natural endowment of the river zone in terms of water transport, soil fertility, and faunal resources. The routing of the main highway through the terra firme interior and the orientation of the feeder roads, all of which are usable year round, to it rather than to the river, assured the spatial segregation of road-induced development from the river zone. The latter, in fact, gained no access to the road network except through the transshipment point of Itacoatiara. The terra firme interior thus obtained much improved access to the markets of both Manaus and Itacoatiara, while the riverine population continued to rely on the more cumbersome and in parts seasonally interrupted river traffic. For the caboclos, relocation along the new road network offered the possibility of escaping traditional dependence on the river trader.

Furthermore, government services were more effective in the road zone. Here land tenure regularization was given priority and property delimitation proved much easier than in the varzea, where boundaries between land and water are fluid and subject to change. EMATER and CEPLAC, the main agricultural extension agencies, devoted far greater attention to the easily accessible road hinterland. These areas could be serviced in single day trips from the city, whereas the river zone required longer, unpredictable, and inconvenient excursions in EMATER's one boat. Refueling points were unreliable, overnight accommodation was primitive, and swarms of mosquitoes and blackflies plagued travellers. Extension personnel were generally more familiar with terra firme agriculture and had little to teach the varzea jute farmers. The extension agents also tended to overestimate the role of flood risk in comparison with the risks inherent in poor soil fertility and the ravages of leafcutter ants on the terra firme. The promotion of tree crops and small animal raising, considered particularly susceptible to flood damage, was thus essentially confined to the road zone.

Because the new infrastructure has been concentrated in the city, it is not surprising that the secondary and tertiary-sector expansion (Table 11) has followed suit, with the exception of one plywood plant, two traditional brick and tile factories in the immediate road hinterland of the city, and some informal sector commercial establishments dispersed in the rural areas. This has produced an extreme concentration of job creation in the city which was previously characterized by endemic unemployment as well as seasonal employment (Smith 1981:27) in the major jute, Brazil nut, cacao, and rubber export establishments, since the latter adjusted their activities to the seasonal supply of raw materials. A large proportion of new jobs assure year-round employment in the lumber industries and the much-expanded urban commerce and services.

Virtually all of the acquisition and development of large and medium-sized rural property has occurred in the previously underoccupied road zone. In contrast, the river zone, an area in which most of the better-endowed locations were already settled and where discontinuous terrain and flooding pose obstacles to large-scale pasture development, was barely affected. Hence new opportunities for rural wage and contract labour, primarily seasonal and unstable because the work was mainly related to the initial land-clearing process, were confined to the road zone.

This major expansion and spatial shift of the municipality's economy in conjunction with improved access to the booming city of Manaus could not fail to produce an acceleration and redirection of intra- and inter-municipal migration. However, the municipality registered no significant net migration gain. Its census population increased to 52,882 from 37,346 during the 1970–1980 period (IBGE 1970b, 1980c), roughly equal to the expected natural increase. Linking Itacoatiara to the national road network did not produce the massive long-distance inmigration common in many other newly accessible areas of the Amazon. Relative remoteness from the Northeast and Centre-South, the principal potential sources of long-distance migrants, the intervening opportunity of more accessible and more dynamic rural frontiers and, particularly, of Manaus, as well as the fact that only relatively poor soils were available for settlement in Itacoatiara largely account for the limited importance of inmigration from distant source areas in the 1970s. In this decade, the municipality's net gain of migrants born outside Amazonas and Pará was a mere 666. A significant part of this inflow was composed of individuals attracted by the expanding public sector and externally controlled private enterprise, notably Fazendas Unidas which contracted labour in the Northeast.

In contrast, the economic boom of Manaus and the improved road produced a net migration loss to the Zona Franca of almost 4,000 persons from all parts of the municipality, that is, more than 10 per cent of the 1970 population. Mass migration to Manaus, which had started with the creation of the Zona Franca and completion of the initial road link in 1967, was heaviest in the early 1970s, with increasing return migration becoming evident at the turn of the decade, when Manaus was affected by national economic problems.

The net outflow to Manaus was roughly equalled by a net inflow of migrants from Pará and other parts of Amazonas. This migrant stream came primarily from small municipalities of the Middle Amazon in which infrastructure development and economic growth had been less than in Itacoatiara. Like the long-distance inmigration, most of this short- and intermediate-distance movement was directed to the City of Itacoatiara and, to a lesser extent, to the road zone. Coming from similar environments, these caboclos, who in 1980 composed half of the local residents born outside the municipality, were not significantly different culturally from the pre-existing population, although they perhaps exhibited a somewhat greater degree of entrepreneurism.

TABLE 11   *Economically Active Population of the Municipality by Sector of Employment, 1970 and 1980*

	1970		1980	
	Persons	Percentage	Persons	Percentage
Primary sector	6,266	67.5	6,056	49.8
Secondary sector	981	10.6	2,103	17.3
Transforming industries	n.a.	n.a.	1,572	12.9
Construction	n.a.	n.a.	409	3.4
Other	n.a.	n.a.	122	1.0
Tertiary sector	2,032	21.9	3,993	32.9
Commerce	499	5.4	752	6.2
Services	573	6.2	1,322	10.9
Transport, communication, storage	301	3.2	466	3.8
Social activities	443	4.8	741	6.1
Public administration	111	1.2	327	2.7
Other	105	1.1	385	3.2
Total	9,279	100.0	12,152	100.0

Source: IBGE 1970b, 1980c.
n.a. not available

Intra-municipal migration, meanwhile, came mainly from the river zone, which experienced an unprecedented series of floods. Most municipal migrants moved from the river to the city and the road zone, but some moved from the road zone to the city. At the same time, a growing proportion of the urban population—which once fluctuated between city and countryside with seasonal employment and unemployment, economic cycles and variable floods—permanently severed its links to the rural area.

The net result of these migration flows is twofold. First, part of the younger and better-educated population, particularly high school graduates, left Itacoatiara for Manaus. This exodus impaired the municipality's capacity to generate locally based modernization. Second, a major intra-municipal demographic shift took place. Although the rural population increased marginally in absolute terms during the 1970s, its representation in the total population declined from 58 to 49 per cent. Concurrently, the proportion of rural population in the road zone jumped from practically nil to approximately 20 per cent.

LAND TENURE CHANGE

The spatial demographic shifts and the selective land acquisition by larger enterprises, both out of state and local, were the principal factors leading to a rapid change in the structure of land tenure during the 1970s. This process and its impact on the pre-existing population, however, differ substantially from the experience of the main settlement frontiers of the Amazon.

First, the existing rural caboclo settlements were relatively dense and occupied a contiguous belt in the river zone. The river environment proved initially unattractive to large enterprise and extra-regional colonists unaccustomed to floodplain conditions. The caboclos of the river zone are essentially peasant farmers practising relatively intensive land use; they are therefore less easily dislodged than the scattered caboclo and Indian populations involved in more extensive land use elsewhere in Amazonia. As a result, traditional patterns of caboclo tenure remained essentially intact in the river zone.

Second, the competition for land in the newly opened road zone lacked the intensity of other frontiers and involved a different set of actors. The local caboclos did not suffer from an acute shortage of land in the river zone; on the contrary, expanding urban opportunities reduced the rural population. Most migrants from other municipalities of Amazonas and western Pará also came from areas where land shortage was not yet a major problem. Leaving relatively remote and underdeveloped areas, they were mainly attracted by Itacoatiara's road access, improving services, and expanding urban opportunities. Most of them moved to the city of Itacoatiara. Colonists from areas with acute land shortage in the Northeast and Centre-South were rare. Thus competition for land in the road zone was primarily between large landowners of local and external origin, often with speculative intentions, and local caboclos or caboclo migrants from the Middle Amazon. The caboclos generally sought to trade small holdings in riverine areas or, if land-less, settlement possibilities in more isolated locations near their areas of origin for larger, and more accessible, properties albeit on relatively poor soils.

The concentration of land tenure in the decade from 1970 to 1980 (Table 12) therefore does not imply the widespread displacement of small farmers as elsewhere in the Amazon, but rather indicates primarily an appro-priation of unclaimed land by large enterprises. In fact, the peasants' access to land improved in absolute terms during the 1970s because the rural popula-tion increased marginally while total land area in farms increased by 74 per cent, from 145,894 to 253,165 hectares (Table 13). The number of mid-sized farms from twenty-five to 99.9 hectares, which were largely controlled by peasants, increased by 69 per cent. At the same time very small properties of less than twenty-five hectares increased by only 14 per cent, probably more because of the addition of small properties in newly settled areas than farm fragmentation (Table 12). The number of farms operated by sharecroppers and tenants decreased substantially in both absolute and relative terms, an indication that these people found alternative opportunities (IBGE 1970a, 1980c). Land-use figures for 1980 indicate that on 70 per cent of farms, fewer than five hectares were under crops and that only 8 per cent of farms grew more than ten hectares of crops (Table 14). These figures also substantiate the assertion that peasants were not facing a significant shortage of land by the end of the 1970s.

If one considers soil quality, however, in the absence of pub-lished figures which might permit a correlation between land capability and tenure, it appears from field observation that quality land is scarce. Virtually all of the better lands, which are essentially confined to the varzea and terra firme fringe, were already occupied by 1970, mainly by small peasant hold-ings. Most additions to the land area in farms have occurred on soil of ques-tionable suitability for crop agriculture.

With regard to spatial differentiation of land tenure, the selec-tive land occupation process of the 1970s has produced three distinct rural zones: (1) the river zone; (2) the western road zone; and (3) the eastern road zone in the immediate road hinterland of the city, roughly delimited by the varzea and the Urubu River (Figure 2). Small peasant holdings continue to dominate the river zone, with great intra-farm environmental diversity and intensive use of the better soils.

In contrast, in the road zone, larger properties dominate even among peasant holders. Peasant settlers generally arrived before or with the large enterprises and initially had access to an abundant supply of public domain. Yet there was no land rush. Colonists gradually occupied land in linear fashion along the new roads and in proximity to roads along intersect-ing water courses. They generally contented themselves with holdings of thirty to one hundred hectares, and neglected to legalize their claims. In the east-ern road zone, which in the 1960s contained some small holdings and a number of properties in the hands of the local elite, a larger percentage of settlers

TABLE 12   *Farms and Area in Farms by Size Category, 1970 and 1980*

Farm Size (hectares)	1970					1980				
	Number of Farms	Percentage of Total Farms	Total Farm Land (hectares)	Percentage of Total Farm Land	Mean size of Farm (hectares)	Number of Farms	Percentage of Total Farms	Total Farm Land (hectares)	Percentage of Total Farm Land	Mean size of Farm (hectares)
up to 4.9	435	16.8	1,134	0.8	2.6	479	14.7	1,382	0.5	2.9
5 – 9.9	386	14.9	2,582	1.8	6.7	413	12.6	2,670	1.0	6.5
10 – 24.9	563	21.8	7,494	5.1	13.3	690	21.1	8,855	3.5	12.8
25 – 49.9	617	23.9	16,648	11.4	27.0	939	28.7	26,263	10.4	28.0
50 – 99.9	223	8.6	13,963	9.6	62.6	478	14.6	28,544	11.3	59.7
100 – 199	156	6.0	19,161	13.1	122.8	150	4.6	18,583	7.3	123.9
200 – 499	154	6.0	39,165	26.9	254.3	74	2.3	20,422	8.1	276.0
500 – 999	33	1.3	19,271	13.2	584.0	13	0.4	9,066	3.6	697.4
1,000 and over	17	0.7	26,477	18.1	1,557.5	34	1.0	137,380	54.3	4,040.6
Total	2,584	100.0	145,895	100.0	56.5	3,270	100.0	253,165	100.0	77.4

Source: Based on IBGE 1970a, 1980a.

TABLE 13   Land Use of Farms, 1970 and 1980

	1970					1980				
	Number of Farms[a]	Percentage of Total Farms	Total Farm Land (hectares)	Percentage of Total Farm Land	Mean size of Farms (hectares)	Number of Farms	Percentage of Total Farms	Total Farm Land (hectares)	Percentage of Total Farm Land	Mean size of Farms (hectares)
Annual crops	2,413	93.4	5,732	3.9	2.4	3,019	92.3	12,150	4.8	4.0
Perennial crops	1,185	45.9	1,957	1.3	1.7	2,082	63.7	5,656	2.2	2.7
Natural pasture	751	29.1	10,277	7.0	13.7	1,106	33.8	14,695	5.8	13.3
Planted pasture	515	19.9	7,470	5.1	14.5	612	18.7	18,661	7.4	30.5
Forest, fallow, unused	2,584	100.0	120,458	82.7	46.6	n.a.	n.a.	202,003	79.8	n.a.
Total of farms/area	2,584	100.0	145,894	100.0	56.5	3,270	100.0	253,165	100.0	77.42

Source: Based on IBGE 1970a, 1980a.
[a]Note multiple counting since a farm may contain several land use categories.
n.a. not available.

acquired modest holdings because proximity to the urban centre permitted more intensive land use. In addition, many of the settlers combined urban employment and residence with small-scale agriculture.

To the consternation of the leadership of the Sindicato dos Trabalhadores Rurais, the caboclos demonstrated few of the attributes of pioneer settlers from South-Central and northeastern Brazil: the hunger for land, the awareness of impending constraints on land availability, and the willingness to brave the interior beyond the existing transport routes. As a result, large enterprise encountered little competition for land in the interior, that is, more than one or two kilometres from transport arteries, and were able to occupy properties with considerable unclaimed frontage along roads and waterways.

Most of the eastern road zone was eventually claimed by the local elite, but much larger holdings were established by extra-regional entrepreneurs in the western road zone. The resulting pattern of tenure in the eastern road zone is characterized by smaller properties than those of the western road zone in both the elite and peasant tenure category. Furthermore, both elite and caboclo tenure categories exhibit a higher proportion of land in agricultural use in the eastern than in the western road zone.

Since the initial occupation of the road zone, a gradual concentration of land tenure has taken place. This phenomenon can be expected to continue as existing large landholders attempt to increase their access to road and river frontage, the latter being important for dry season pasture and water for the expanding livestock herds. Forceful eviction has been rare

TABLE 14   *Farms by Area under Crops, 1970 and 1980*

Area under crops (hectares)	1970		1980	
	Number of Farms	Percentage of Total Farm Land	Number of Farms	Percentage of Total Farm Land
0	97	3.8	104	3.2
0.1 – 0.9	96	3.7	64	2.0
1 – 1.9	596	23.1	460	14.1
2 – 4.9	1,415	54.8	1,660	50.8
5 – 9.9	331	12.8	724	22.1
10 – 19.9	41	1.6	184	5.6
20 – 49.9	5	0.2	55	1.7
50 – 99.9	1	0.0	8	0.2
100 – 199	2	0.1	5	0.2
200 – 499	—	—	4	0.1
500 – 1000	—	—	2	0.1
Total	2,584	100.1[a]	3,270	100.1

Source: Based on IBGE 1970a, 1980a.
[a]Totals are more than 100 per cent because of rounding.

because the caboclos, in an environment of expanding alternative opportunities, have thus far shown considerable readiness to sell their land under minor inducements. Meanwhile, there is little evidence of attempts to establish new large holdings in areas already fully claimed.

AGRICULTURAL CREDIT

Apart from the spontaneous process of land settlement, the introduction in the mid-1970s of highly subsidized crop production credit by BB, BEA and BASA was the main agent of change for the rural population. Credit availability increased substantially only during the period of 1978-1980, then decreased sharply in 1981.

As noted in Chapter 2, within the local context, the crop credit program had the potential of achieving two major effects. First, it could have increased peasant production, in turn creating broad multiplier effects through increased peasant demand, processing of crops, and increased availability of food for local consumption. Second, universal peasant access to formal credit could have modernized the local social structure by undermining the traditional patron-client relationship.

If some progress was made toward the achievement of these goals, it was hardly due to the coherent implementation of the credit program. In fact, peasants with little credit experience, accustomed to a patron-client relationship where most transactions were in kind, were swamped by a wave of cheap money which the banks disbursed with scant supervision and very little understanding of the workings of the peasant production system. In the illustrative case of the Banco do Brasil, which handles the bulk of the crop credit, ten agents, including bank, EMATER and CEPLAC personnel, were struggling valiantly in 1980 to carry out field inspection and extension service for 7,181 loans supposedly involving 65,270 hectares (Table 15). Even under optimum operating conditions, this would have been an impossible task. Given inadequate transport, non-existent soil information, the difficulties of inspecting densely vegetated, often muddy, terrain on generally unsurveyed properties, and numerous other problems, it was a nightmare. Yet the inability to monitor credit effectively did not significantly limit its availability.

The bulk of the credit did reach the target peasant population, if only because few larger landholders were involved in crop farming. In this respect, credit did represent a broad-spread infusion into the local economy. Long deprived, unaccustomed to having ready cash and, as will be seen shortly, with limited options for productive investment, the peasants went on a spending spree for basic consumer goods. These involved processed foods, apparel, household utensils, and modest extravagances such as bicycles, radios, and tape decks. The urban retail trade was the main beneficiary. Since peasants were obliged to come to the city to collect loan installments, it was natural that they made most major purchases immediately after leaving the bank. Often they incurred additional debt with the retailers, expecting to repay it with subsequent crop credit installments.

TABLE 15   *Banco do Brasil Crop Loans and Hectares Financed, 1978-1980*

| | Loans | | | | | | | | Hectares Financed | | | | | | | | Hectares per Loan |
| | 1978 | | 1979 | | 1980 | | 1978-1980 | | 1978 | | 1979 | | 1980 | | 1978-1980 | | 1978-1980 |
	No.	%	No.	%	No.	%	No.	%	No.	%	No.	%	No.	%	No.	%	
Jute & malva	841	64.3	1,474	68.0	2,514	35.0	4,829	45.3	8,884	75.0	15,221	76.5	17,890	27.4	41,995	43.3	8.7
Manioc	381	29.2	506	23.3	2,613	36.4	3,500	32.8	2,505	21.2	3,357	16.8	34,338	52.6	40,180	41.4	11.5
Beans	10	0.8	16	0.7	958	13.3	984	9.2	27	0.2	110	0.6	6,296	9.7	6,433	6.6	6.5
Bananas	6	0.4	1	0.0	715	10.0	722	6.8	44	0.4	5	0.0	3,275	5.0	3,324	3.4	4.6
Pineapples	1	0.1	60	2.8	142	2.0	203	1.9	12	0.1	299	1.5	540	0.8	851	0.9	4.2
Maize	12	0.9	62	2.9	42	0.6	116	1.1	60	0.5	455	2.3	273	0.4	788	0.8	6.8
Rubber	—	—	1	0.0	81	1.1	82	0.8	—	—	15	0.1	2,090	3.2	2,105	2.2	25.7
Rice	10	0.8	19	0.9	32	0.4	61	0.6	57	0.5	125	0.6	171	0.3	353	0.4	5.8
Guaraná	18	1.4	13	0.6	26	0.4	57	0.5	170	1.4	221	1.1	272	0.4	663	0.7	11.6
Cacao	23	1.8	15	0.7	10	0.1	48	0.5	74	0.6	106	0.5	10	0.0	190	0.2	4.0
Watermelons	3	0.2	—	—	18	0.3	21	0.2	10	0.1	—	—	45	0.1	55	0.1	2.6
Tomatoes	2	0.1	—	—	17	0.2	19	0.2	2	0.0	—	—	23	0.0	25	0.0	1.3
Vegetables	—	—	2	0.1	13	0.2	15	0.1	—	—	4	0.0	47	0.1	51	0.1	3.4
Total	1,307	100.0	2,169	100.0	7,181	100.0	10,657	100.0	11,845	100.0	19,898	100.0	65,270	100.0	97,013	100.1[a]	9.1

Source: Derived from unpublished data of Banco do Brasil. Data apply to the area serviced by BB's Itacoatiara office; i.e., Itacoatiara and 4 neighbouring municipalities.

[a]Total is more than 100 per cent due to rounding.

A further infusion into the urban economy resulted from the fact that part of the urban elite sought and obtained crop credit. The eagerness of urbanites to become "crop farmers" is not surprising because crop credit was far cheaper than any other line of bank credit and its use was not effectively monitored. Access to crop credit by the urban elite was facilitated by the fact that many of its members already owned rural property. Others hastily acquired land to qualify. Though some bona fide crop projects were submitted for financing and were partly executed, the main objective of the urban elite was to divert capital to urban investments and such other purposes as land purchase and pasture expansion. Large sums of crop credit were used to expand the retail inventory in response to actual and expected increases in consumer demand resulting from crop credit.

Misappropriation of credit for other purposes than the production inputs for which it was intended was only one of the factors reducing expected production increases as a result of the credit program. Constraints bearing on the production system itself were equally important. First, the amount of credit allocated per hectare specified in the loan contract was generally inadequate to purchase required inputs at market prices. Thus, even where bona fide producers did use the bulk of their loan for inputs, these were normally applied to a smaller area than specified in the contract.

Second, purchased inputs were in short supply or relatively unattractive to peasant producers. Most important, landless rural labour was scarce due to rural outmigration and increased peasant access to land during the 1970s. Modern inputs were costly and not always available when required. Furthermore, an adequate return on their use was by no means assured because of the insufficient control of their application by the extension service, environmental risks, and low as well as unpredictable crop prices. Thus the peasant farmers, who constituted the mass of credit recipients actually growing crops, continued to rely primarily on family labour and on the use of traditional techniques.

The gross overestimation of peasant land-use capacity by the credit program is evident from a comparison of crop area per farm reported in the 1980 census (Table 14) and hectares specified per BB loan (Table 15), particularly if one considers that many peasants managed to obtain multiple loans. Some 70 per cent of farms recorded in the 1980 census had fewer than five hectares under crops. A further 22 per cent cultivated less than ten hectares. Yet the mean number of hectares specified per BB loan in 1978-80 was 9.1 hectares, a figure reasonably representative of loans to peasants, as illustrated by the following data for the two principal crops financed. In the case of jute "mini" and "small" loan projects, to use BB terminology, the land to be cultivated averaged 5.0 and 8.7 hectares respectively. The corresponding figures for manioc were 9.2 and 13.1 hectares (unpublished BB data for 1978-1980).

The disparity between reality and bank projections is even more striking if the aggregate data on crop area are compared. In the 1980 census, the total crop surface reported by farmers in Itacoatiara amounted to 17,806 hectares (Table 13). Meanwhile, BB claimed to have financed 65,270 hectares of crops (Table 15) within the five municipalities serviced from its Itacoatiara office, at least half of which must be attributed to the municipality of Itacoatiara. One must remember that two other banks, BEA and BASA, disbursed crop credit—albeit on a lesser scale—and that not every farmer took loans.

While the credit-induced expansion of crop area envisaged by the banks was highly unrealistic, some increase in crop production doubtless did result from bank credit, though data confirming this are unavailable. The increase in overall crop production attributable to credit must have been minor, inasmuch as the bulk of peasant labour would have been allocated to cropping in any case. However, the direct use of crop credit for the purchase of consumer goods did encourage a reallocation of labour from diverse subsistence activities to crops targetted by the credit program.

Thus the eminence of jute in the varzea and manioc on the terra firme was re-inforced by a local credit policy which consistently allocated most of the credit to these crops (Table 15). Bankers, extension agents and peasants alike considered them the least problematic options: they were familiar to the peasants, did not depend on modern inputs, involved little environmental risk, and appeared to have good market prospects. Much more limited progress was made with regard to perennials, including rubber, guaraná, cacao, and bananas. In the case of cacao and bananas, however, the new plantings did not even compensate for the loss and spoilage of acreage in the varzea occasioned by the three heavy floods of the 1970s. There was little peasant response to a temporary surge of credit for beans, which faced too many difficulties with regard to disease, productivity, and storage in both the varzea and terra firme. A short-lived promotion of pineapples was abandoned when plans for a processing plant collapsed. With the exception of manioc, bananas, and beans, food crops were not promoted and production of most of the local subsistence crops stagnated or declined.

With regard to the production and multiplier effects of the credit program, one must conclude that results were mixed. Overall crop production increased, but food production—with the exception of manioc—stagnated. No new agricultural processing plants were established. Multiplier effects benefitting the urban retail sector were strong, but did not take the form envisaged by the credit program. The demand for production inputs increased only moderately, while the bulk of credit was used directly for the acquisition of consumer goods. Since little cumulative capitalization of crop farms took place, except for some investment in perennials, it is questionable whether the initial surge of peasant demand for urban goods and services could be sustained without continuous infusions of further credit. In 1981 the instability of crop-credit-based economic growth was demonstrated when low jute prices and reduced credit availability curtailed peasant demand, leaving many retailers overstocked.

The credit program did achieve considerable success in loosening the traditional patron-client relationship, particularly in the road zone, which lacked the well-established network of rural traders and offered more flexible means of access to urban markets. For many river zone caboclos, however, it was difficult to break a stable personal relationship with a patrão, which involved security as much as exploitation, even when the patrão did not have the leverage of accumulated debt to maintain control over his clients.

As new or additional patrons, the banks exerted less influence over their clients than had traditional intermediaries. Since the banks were unable to monitor or direct the production process, they had little control over the use of credit. In the absence of government marketing agencies, the banks had no comprehensive mechanism to assure credit repayment through control over crop deliveries. Only the cooperative (CMAI) had an agreement with the banks to discount outstanding debts from crop deliveries, a factor which helps explain the low proportion of the members using its marketing services. Finally, the banks showed no serious inclination, in the short term, to foreclose on defaulting debtors. In these circumstances, it was inevitable that credit recipients, unaccustomed to financial management and planning, were likely to overextend themselves financially even more than they had in traditional patron-client relationships.

The availability of bank credit permitted the peasant to bypass the rural trader and get consumer goods and production inputs directly from the expanding urban retail sector. In many cases this entailed new forms of debt dependence on urban retailers.

It proved far more difficult to dislodge the rural traders' control over the marketing of agricultural products in the river zone. In many areas they monopolized both the boats able to handle bulk cargo and crop-storage facilities. The cooperative, with its infrequent boat service and lack of rural storage depots, was not yet a reliable substitute, nor could it fully compete with the traders' more flexible disbursement of cash to producers upon (or before) crop delivery. Nevertheless, an increasing number of peasants managed to deal directly with the cooperative or the other urban export establishments, often by contracting boat transport individually or in coordination with neighbours.

Some traditional traders who were normally involved in farming themselves managed to obtain crop credit and apply it to their trading activities. Furthermore, a number of astute farmers in the river zone used part of their crop credit to establish themselves as intermediaries by financing and purchasing jute production among neighbours unable or unwilling to negotiate bank loans themselves. This misuse of crop credit contributed to the increasing role of "capitalists," decried by STR in the cooperative.

On balance, however, crop credit has strengthened the independence of peasant producers and given them a wider range of choices. Whether these achievements can be maintained in the long term is open to question in view of reduced availability of bank credit and increased interest rates since 1981. An additional consideration is the difficulties many peasants with accumulated debt face in getting new bank loans.

The crop credit program has had major implications for the structure of land tenure. Access to credit was contingent on documented ownership of land. For the financing of annual crops, the banks officially required legal title or the Licença de Ocupação (LO), a provisional legal document issued by the government land agencies upon survey and verification of effective land occupancy. For smaller loans, however, the banks often contented themselves with proof of registration of holdings for tax purposes with the local cadastral office of INCRA or with the privately managed local land registry office, the Cartório. These registrations are based solely on the declaration of the registrant, are not verified, and are not recognized as legal documentation of tenure. In contrast, the banks insisted on definitive titles before awarding loans for perennials, which generally involve longer commitments and larger sums than annual crops.

This link between cheap crop credit and documented tenure necessarily produced an increase in the value of formally documented holdings. A wave of new registrations ensued at INCRA's cadastral office and the Cartório, while INCRA and ITERAM were slow to issue new LOs and definitive titles. Expectation of comprehensive tenure legalization by the land agencies upon completion of the extensive archival search and field visits which occupied them in the late 1970s only heightened the demand for some kind of formal documentation of de facto tenure. Furthermore, rural holdings up to one rural module, that is, one hundred hectares in the Amazon, were exempted from the rural land tax in 1979, thus removing a major impediment to voluntary land registration. As a result, the INCRA cadaster alone was flooded with 2,015 new registrations between October 1980 and August 1981 (INCRA, personal communication), an increase of 55 per cent.

The progressive formalization of tenure and the increased demand for documented land holdings affected peasant tenure in several ways. First, it restricted the availability of unclaimed land and reduced the tendency toward informal transactions of land and use rights which had prevailed when land was valued only as a means of production. Second, it encouraged conflict between claimants, given the disorderly nature of the registration process. Finally, and perhaps most importantly, it served as an inducement for land sales, especially where shortsighted caboclos with legal title faced attractive offers from an urban elite eager to acquire holdings which would open access to crop credit, or where peasants sought escape from an unmanageable debt burden.

Thus, although credit doubtless helped many peasants consolidate their farming operations, it also contributed to peasant withdrawal from farming, particularly while alternative opportunities in the expanding economy still appeared attractive. At the same time, the traditional ability of return migrants to re-integrate through peasant farming was increasingly restricted. This was made clear to caboclos returning from Manaus when the Zona Franca economy started to stagnate at the turn of the decade.

CHANGING USE OF NATURAL RESOURCES

Although the major instruments intended for the transformation of the rural sector—credit, extension services, and SUDAM incentives—produced results which fell short of expectations, the 1970s were a decade of unprecedented change in the utilization of resources. Expansion of agricultural areas, increased lumber exploitation, and the consolidation of a commercial fishing industry were the main manifestations of this change. The quality of resource use did not improve significantly, however, even in the agricultural sector, which received most of the government's attention. Whether the changes represent progress toward long-term economic and environmental stability is questionable.

Agricultural resource use

Census data indicate that the area in agricultural use doubled from 1970 to 1980 (Table 16). Nevertheless, in 1980, 80 per cent of the area in farms and 92 per cent of the municipality's land area remained under forest. Because the census does not provide consistent breakdowns by sub-zone, property size, or specific crops, field observations made in 1981 are used here to interpret changes in the major categories of land use.

The bulk of agricultural expansion took place on the terra firme close to the new road network. This applies particularly to planted pasture, which overtook natural pasture to become the main agricultural land use category in Itacoatiara. Large and medium-sized properties account for most of the planted pasture increase because few of the family farmers who settled in the road zone managed to become cattle raisers. The quality of planted pasture is generally poor to begin with, and is often permitted to deteriorate substantially with time, particularly on large, absentee-owned enterprises.

TABLE 16   *Change in Farm Land Use, 1970 and 1980*

	1970		1980		Increase 1970-1980
	hectares	%	hectares	%	%
Crops	7,689	5.2	17,805	7.0	131.6
Annual crops	5,732	3.9	12,150	4.8	112.0
Perennial crops	1,957	1.3	5,656	2.2	189.0
Pasture	17,747	12.1	33,356	13.2	88.0
Natural pasture	10,277	7.0	14,695	5.8	43.0
Planted pasture	7,470	5.1	18,661	7.4	149.8
Total in agricultural use	25,436	17.3	51,162	20.2	101.1
Forest, fallow, unused	120,458	82.7	202,003	79.8	67.7
Total area in farms	145,894	100.0	253,165	100.0	73.5

Source: Based on Table 7.

Natural pasture, which in Itacoatiara is mainly on seasonally flooded varzea land, also increased substantially, albeit less than planted pasture (Table 16). This increase may have been somewhat inflated at the expense of planted pasture because of incorrect enumeration of degraded planted pasture. The increased utilization of natural varzea pasture involved a wider range of property sizes. These included, on the one hand, large and medium-sized properties in the road zone and extending into the varzea, particularly along the northern tributaries of the Amazon and, on the other, river-zone family farmers who boarded the cattle of terra firme ranchers during the dry season or who managed to acquire a few head of cattle themselves.

The mean density of livestock on natural and planted pasture combined remained stable at one head per hectare, suggesting that pasture management changed little during the 1970s. Given the poor quality of planted terra firme pasture, the increased use of natural varzea pasture is largely a function of the expanded terra firme livestock herds, which require supplementary pasture during the dry season because other sources of supplementary feed are uneconomical. By the early 1980s, most of the natural pasture surface in the varzea had been put to use. It must be expected that, if terra firme ranchers continue to expand their herds, they will put pressure on varzea farmers to convert cropland to pasture.

While pastures expanded by 88 per cent during the decade, the crop area registered an even more dramatic increase of 132 per cent—albeit from a smaller base figure (Table 16). This represents an increase to 0.68 from 0.36 hectares in the cropland surface per capita of the rural population. The bulk of the increase in perennial crops (Table 16)—mainly rubber and, to a lesser extent, cacao, guaraná, and Brazil nuts—occurred on large and medium-sized properties. However, the fact that the proportion of farms reporting perennial crops increased to 64 from 46 per cent during the decade indicates that a broad range of farmers participated. The increased area in annual crops, in contrast, is mainly attributable to peasant producers. Only one large estate, the sugar cane plantation of Fazendas Unidas, is significantly involved in annual crops.

Table 14 illustrates that a large proportion of peasant producers expanded the area under annual crops on their farms. If the categories of 0.1 to twenty hectares of cropland are considered representative of the range of family farms, notable shifts have occurred. The number of farms with less than two hectares of crops declined in both absolute and relative terms. An intermediate category of two to five hectares increased in absolute terms, and farms with more than five hectares of annual crops registered strong gains in both absolute and relative terms.

This increase in cropland, mainly involving annual crops on family farms, is attributable to two main factors. First, it results from the progressive integration of the peasantry into the market economy under the impact of credit and extension service, as well as improved market access and diversification of marketing channels. Second, it reflects the relative shift from the intensive, selective land use of the varzea to more extensive forms of land use on the terra firme. The latter is characterized by poorer soils, larger property size, and the consideration that, in the absence of titles, property values and land tenure security increase with area cleared.

The explosive growth of pasture and cropland was not accompanied by corresponding innovations in the use of land. Use of modern production inputs was limited and land productivity stagnated. The density of livestock on pasture remained unchanged at one head per hectare (IBGE 1970, 1980a). Overall crop productivity per unit area even declined, in conjunction with the relative shift of cropland to poorer terra firme soils.

Nor was there any significant change in cropping patterns. The main innovation was the introduction of tree crops, principally rubber, to some of the road zone farms. Generally the conservatism of the caboclos conspired with the expediency of bank and extension personnel in favour of well-established local crops, two of which accounted for two-thirds of the area in annual crops. In 1980 jute and malva, the traditional export crops, represented 47 per cent of the total surface under annual crops and were grown on 74 per cent of all farms. Manioc, the traditional regional staple, took up 19 per cent of the annual crop surface and was reported by 61 per cent of farms. The third annual crop, maize, more than doubled its area in the 1970s, in spite of being neglected by credit and extension programs. In 1980 it constituted 7 per cent of the area in annual crops and was present on 30 per cent of the municipality's farms.

In contrast, less than 1 per cent of farms reported rice, a national staple which is gaining importance in comparison to manioc in most of the colonization areas and which appears suited to varzea conditions (Barrow 1985; Malafaia et al. 1969). Other non-traditional products such as tomatoes and vegetables fared equally poorly. This lack of diversification is particularly striking in view of ready access to the expanding and diversifying Manaus market and in comparison with the Japanese colony Efigenio Salles, which is located along the Itacoatiara-Manaus road barely outside the municipal boundary, and which supplies Manaus with a range of vegetables and fruits.

Lumber extraction

In conjunction with agriculture, lumbering experienced a major upswing in the 1970s. This upswing followed a period of stagnation because of the near-total exhaustion of easily accessible timber in the river zone of Itacoatiara. The surge is obviously related to road construction and agricultural land clearing in the road zone. The favourable location between Manaus and the expanding lumber-processing industries of Itacoatiara permitted the exploitation of a broader range of species than are economically viable in most of Amazonia because of the distance to markets.

Nevertheless, a number of factors constrained the full utilization of these newly accessible lumber resources. Most importantly, the industries in Itacoatiara had a longstanding link to a vast fluvial hinterland where established intermediaries organized bulk supply.[10] The same applies to Manaus. In 1981 none of the processing plants of Itacoatiara obtained a major part of its raw material from the road zone (Elite Survey 1981), where large contractors were slow to establish themselves. In addition, demand from these industries was irregular because they faced labour, management, and export market difficulties.

Thus the demand for road zone lumber was not as strong, nor as regular, as its favourable location between two major urban-industrial market centres would suggest. The supply of lumber was abundant in the road zone because extensive areas were being cleared for pastures and crops. In these circumstances major landholders, able to offer large, contiguous surfaces for exploitation, were in a better position than small holders to attract lumbering contractors, or to manage the extraction process themselves. Small holders, in contrast, often had to offer concessional terms to attract contractors.

Generally, lumbering remained a peripheral activity of land clearing, rarely extending significantly beyond the areas being cleared for agriculture. It doubtless helped to subsidize the land-clearing process, especially for larger landholders, yet its contribution to capital accumulation and employment among the rural population was minimal. In the road zone, fewer than 2 per cent of farm households had sold lumber in a twelve-month period 1980–1981, and barely 4 per cent of heads of household in the road zone identified forest extraction, including lumbering, as their (main) occupation (Survey 1981).

Commercial fishing

While lumbering became the dominant, albeit minor, form of commercial resource extraction in the road zone, commercial fishing assumed similar prominence in the river zone. Commercial fishing boats operating in the area originated in Itacoatiara and downriver ports as well as in Manaus, where the registered fleet grew from 135 in 1970 to 728 in 1980 (Junk 1983:74). Because only a small number of local boat owners and contracted fishermen were involved, the direct contribution of commercial fishing to the local economy was even more limited than that of lumber.

Two factors facilitated the encroachment of commercial fishermen into an area previously dominated by subsistence fishing and small-scale, local-market-oriented fishing. First, because most of the commercial fishing vessels were small motorboats outfitted with an ice chest, they depended on a ready local supply of ice and freezing facilities to prepare fish for transshipment to external markets. While the nearest ice supply was in Manaus, the local commercial fishery for external markets was limited to a few larger

---

10. Industries in Itacoatiara City identified the following supply areas: Novo Aripuaná, Manicoré, Humaitá, and Rondônia on the Madeira River; Coari, Tefé, and São Paulo de Olivença on the Solimões; as well as the Purús and Juruá, tributaries of the Solimões (Elite Survey 1981).

vessels with extended range. The situation changed in the early 1970s, when Itacoatiara upgraded its power supply, permitting the installation of an ice factory in 1973 and a fish freezing plant in 1975 (Table 9). Of similar importance was the paved highway, which permitted refrigerated trucking to the expanding Manaus market, where much of the population continued to rely on fish for the bulk of its protein intake. Furthermore, fish could be trucked to South-Central Brazil, where freshwater fish from local sources were growing scarce because of overexploitation and pollution.

In the Itacoatiara area (as in most of the Amazon), commercial fishing did not differ substantially from subsistence fishing in terms of technology, and spatial and seasonal patterns. Both employed a range of simple instruments described by Smith (1981:37-82), including simple seine and gill nets. Commercial boat owners contracted fishermen who fished from canoes in the immediate vicinity of the contractor's boat. This technology is relatively ineffective in the main river and in conditions of large-scale flooding which disperse fish populations. Thus fishing focused on spatially and seasonally concentrated fish resources. These are encountered in lakes during the low-water season and at the mouths of *paranás* (side channels) and small tributaries of the main river at the time of seasonal fish migrations.

Spatial and seasonal concentration made the impact of commercial fishing considerable, in spite of its low technology. Furthermore commercial and subsistence fishing were placed in direct competition for a locally concentrated resource in well-defined traditional community fishing grounds.

Meanwhile the pressure on fish stocks—and the potential for conflict—also increased within caboclo communities. This was partly due to the fact that a number of community members were enticed into commercial fishing. Also, the example of commercial fishermen eroded the fear of supernatural creatures, such as the giant watersnake ("cobra grande") which was still given credence by 85 per cent of Itacoatiara fishermen in 1977 (Smith 1981:107), thus removing taboos which once protected certain areas from exploitation.

Government regulation did little to halt conflicts and destructive resource use. Legislation dating from the 1930s permitting commercial fishing by outsiders in all "navigable" waters proved unsuited for the protection of community fishing grounds, even in backwaters of seasonal or dubious navigability (Smith 1981:123). Restrictions of timing, minimum size, and quantity of catch were not only based on inadequate scientific knowledge of fish ecology but had limited effect due to insufficient control. To the extent that they were enforced, they could raise new obstacles for subsistence fishermen who relied on the occasional sale of part of their catch for survival.

Implications of the changing use of resources

Overall, the direct economic benefits of the dynamically expanding use of resources and associated urban multiplier effects did reach a broad spectrum of the local population, although they were unequally shared.

These short-term economic gains, however, were achieved at the expense of a destabilized relationship between local society and its resource environment. Government provided the necessary infrastructure and some incentives for increased resource use, but failed to regulate resource exploitation and did little to encourage local processing of raw materials.

Few direct benefits were derived by the local population from the commercial exploitation of lumber and fish. In contrast, the bulk of the rural population was involved in, and gained economically from, the expansion of agriculture. Much of this economic gain, however, was ephemeral or artificial, involving subsidized credit, temporary employment in land clearing, and land sale. The main multiplier effects of growth in the primary sector occurred in the urban service and construction sector through increased rural demand and capital transfer from the countryside.

Industrial development related to local primary resource development was limited. The lumber-processing industries which accounted for the bulk of industrial growth since 1970 were only marginally dependent on local resources—with the exception of the short-lived sawmill of Mil Madereira, which relied completely on local supply. None of the other mills listed the municipality among their major source areas (Elite Survey 1981). The four main industries handling local agricultural products (Brasiljuta, Sabba, Cooperativa Mista, Correia) expanded capacity and employment to some extent. They did not, however, implement a single innovation which departed from the traditional pattern of storage and minimal processing required to prepare raw materials for shipment. No further establishments were added, and the Guaraná Rio Negro softdrink bottling plant closed its doors by 1985. The ice and freezing plants, with a combined employment of forty-one (Table 9), were the only industrial establishments owing their existence to the commercial fishery, although they also served a heterogeneous urban and riverboat clientele.

These inputs into the local economy of accelerated resource utilization must be weighed against an increasingly unbalanced relationship between local society and its resource base. Much primary sector growth was achieved through expansion into and increased dependence on the terra firme, where a combination of marginal soils, high cost inputs, poor support systems, caboclo and large landholder conservatism as well as speculative attitudes, have combined to preclude intensive and sustainable land uses in the majority of cases. Lumber resources as well as Brazil nut stands and wildlife on which caboclos relied for income or dietary supplements were largely destroyed in the process. And, in the long run, the low quality of terra firme pastures may well require the conversion of varzea croplands to sustain the terra firme livestock herds.

In the varzea, the critical resource issue is declining fish stocks,[11] given the crucial dietary function of fish and the role of fishing as an income supplement and pastime in local caboclo society. Caboclos blame

---

11. The local population reports that fish stocks have declined substantially since the early 1970s. No systematic monitoring of fish stocks has taken place in the area.

the encroachment of predatory commercial fishing. Numerous conflicts over local fishing grounds have taken place between commercial fishermen and caboclo communities. Furthermore, it may be assumed that the expansion of cleared land in the varzea, and particularly the encroachment of pasture, jute and malva into areas subject to seasonal inundation, has affected the reproduction and feeding patterns of many species of fish.

A final destabilizing trend, promoted by the ready availability of targetted crop credit, is the growing specialization of rural producers, particularly at the expense of subsistence activities.

In general terms, the changes of man-environment relationships represent a new, accelerated phase in the long-term erosion of caboclo society's diversified use of the rich and complementary resource system contained in varzea, river, and terra firme. In the absence of effective government controls and relief programs, the move toward dependence on terra firme, specialized integration into the market economy, decline of certain resources, and eventual competition between crop farmers and livestock raisers puts rural caboclo society increasingly at risk.

Reactions by the caboclo community to the erosion of its traditional resource relationships have generally been fragmentary and ad hoc. Only the encroachment of commercial fishing brought about a rapid, widespread, and sustained reaction because subsistence fishing was directly and very visibly threatened. Not only do commercial fishermen encroach on previously uncontested traditional community fishing grounds, but they fish in full view of caboclo settlements, which are often concentrated along the strategic passages in questions. There have been strong and occasionally violent caboclo reactions against the outsiders. In many cases, caboclos have succeeded in protecting lesser water bodies from outside encroachment. Also, there has been conflict in some communities when members tried to convert to specialized commercial fishing.

The institutions defending caboclo interests, that is, the Church and STR, have fundamentally, but so far ineffectually, questioned the direction of change in the system of resource use. Indicative of this position is the Church's refusal to provide land to the prefecture for constructing a fishing terminal and some STR members' advocacy of a return to diversified agriculture instead of excessive dependence on jute.

4. LAND AND LABOUR: TRENDS AND PROSPECTS IN PERCEPTION AND BEHAVIOUR

To evaluate the impact of the changing roles of the various internal and external actors and the transformation of environmental relationships on the behaviour and perception of the population, the research team conducted a representative sample survey in the three distinct zones of the municipality in August 1981 (Figure 5).[12] The survey benefitted from the recently completed 1980 census, which provided basic demographic information disaggregated for the municipality's forty-seven enumeration districts. On this basis, a disproportionate stratified random sample was drawn. The sample (N = 575, 6.8 per cent of heads of household) was weighted to ensure sufficient representation of the two rural environments: the river zone (N = 200, 6.3 per cent), the road zone (N = 177, 16 per cent), and the city, which contains slightly more than half of the municipality's population (N = 198, 4.7 per cent). For purposes of analysis, the road zone was, in turn, divided into road zone 1 (N = 77), the most recently settled area between Urubú and Prêto rivers, and road zone 2 (N = 100), the immediate hinterland of the city up to the first Urubú River crossing. The questionnaire contained sixty-eight questions and resulted in a data set with 122 variables. These data are discussed in this chapter to explain the past dynamics of migration, land ownership, work, and problems, and as a basis for understanding likely trends in the future.

Before turning to the analysis of the data, it is useful to recall that the post-1970 changes discussed in chapters 2 and 3 represent a broadened range of opportunities for the rural and urban population of Itacoatiara. It should also be noted that the continuing availability of land in the river zone, which did not initially attract large landholders, and expanded availability of land in the road zone, may mean that the local peasantry does not yet feel land pressures. Also, when considering the perceptions of the population, it should not be forgotten that this is an area occupied by caboclos who have been variously characterized as "in movement," "atomized," and "unstable" (for example, Moran 1974; Parker 1985). Thus the opportunities, as well as the threats, facing local society are mediated by a set of perceptual criteria which may well define the situation differently for the caboclo than for the Northeasterner, let alone the Southerner, in the same situation.

---

12. Because of problems of accessibility and lack of cooperation on the part of some large enterprises, the sample for the road zone includes a small portion of the neighbouring municipality of Silves, whose history and characteristics are similar to adjacent parts of Itacoatiara.

FIGURE 5   *Itacoatiara-Silves: Survey Areas*

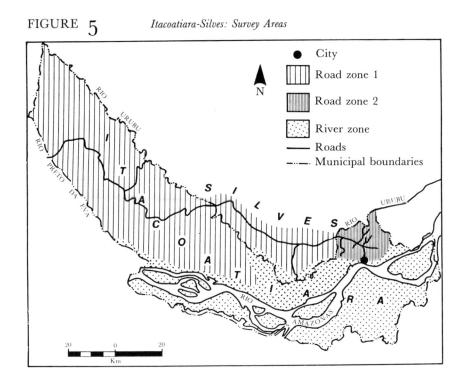

MIGRATION

The penchant of the caboclo "to move from one locality to another, seeking always to improve his economic situation" (Moran 1974:142) is confirmed by the data for Itacoatiara. If intra-municipal moves are included, a significantly higher migration rate emerges than depicted in the census migration data discussed in Chapter 3, which consider only inter-municipal migration. Some 68 per cent of respondents were migrants. The majority had migrated more than once. In the road zone, the rate of previous migration reached 91 per cent, in the city 64 per cent. These rates are not surprising, because the road zone was only recently opened to settlement and the city, as the local growth centre, was the focus of rural urban migration. More striking, and indicative of the casual nature of caboclo migration, is the fact that even in the river zone, recently drained by intra-municipal migration as well as outmigration to Manaus, 52 per cent of respondents had migrated before, and a majority had done so more than once.

It seems clear that, before the time of the survey, a shortage of land was not, or at least was not perceived to be, a major migration determinant. Only 12 per cent of former migrants identified lack of land, in quantitative or qualitative terms, as the principal motive for their last migration

(Table 17). Sixty per cent cited general, fairly vague reasons for their last move, which is in line with what is known about caboclo society. So far, then, the pressure on the land is not recognized by most of the population in the municipality as a major cause of their fairly frequent migrations.

TABLE **17** *Principal Motive Cited for Leaving Last Place of Residence*

Motive	Percentage
Seeking general improvement	32
Brought by friends or relatives	28
Lack of land	12
Lack of work	10
Seeking better services	9
Desire for independent work	6
Other	3
Total	100

Note: N = 391

Further data from the survey give an overall picture of relative satisfaction with the present location and a declared intention to remain. For example, when asked to compare their present situation with that in their last place of residence, those who had migrated at least once (N = 391) reported as follows: 76 per cent were better off, 8 per cent were worse off, and 16 per cent were the same. A comparison of change in family situation reveals that migrants are more successful than non-migrants: over the preceding five years, 59 per cent of migrants, but only 40 per cent of non-migrants indicate improvement. The whole sample was asked whether they intended to remain at the present location or move on. Of those who had never moved, some 94 per cent reported they intended to remain; 84 per cent of those having moved at least once indicated their intention to remain. One may conclude, then, that people are satisfied where they are, at least for the moment, and overwhelmingly intend to remain. As much as anything, this signifies the temporary absence of acute problems and lack of clear alternatives. From the literature on caboclo society, as well as the data discussed in the last chapter, it seems likely that more people will move than declared this intention at the time of the survey.

LAND TENURE AND CONFLICT

Although only 12 per cent of previous migrants reported that lack of land, in terms of quality or quantity, was the cause for their last move, some data suggest that the lack of land is increasingly important as a reason for migration. Overall, seventy-five respondents or 13 per cent, reported that they intended to move on. This rate varied as follows: road zone 1, 30 per cent; road zone 2, 11 per cent; city, 8 per cent; and river zone, 13 per cent.

Some 24 per cent of this subsample gave as their reason lack of land; among those who had migrated once or more, twice as many gave this reason for their last move. Further, this figure varies from 16 per cent in the river zone, where the encroachment of large enterprise remains limited, to an average of 40 per cent in the two road zones, where pressure is increasing. It is highest in road zone 2, with 46 per cent. Here, there is indeed more pressure due to purchases of land by local owners who are more actively developing their land than the largely absentee owners of road zone 1.

As yet there have been few perceived conflicts over land owner-ship, although the respondents may not have recognized what was in fact going on. Of the 344 respondents who reported that they owned land in the rural areas, 85 per cent indicated that they had not been involved in con-flicts. Of the conflicts reported by the remaining 15 per cent, or fifty respond-ents, approximately 42 per cent might be considered caused by pressure by large landowners. The other 58 per cent centred on problems involving small farmers. However, in line with the data on the declared intention to move due to a lack of land, the average of 15 per cent involved in conflicts breaks down into 14 per cent in the river zone, 9 per cent in road zone 1, where partial land regularization by INCRA preceded the survey, and a high of 26 per cent in road zone 2. There is, then, some evidence of conflicts and outmigration due to land scarcity, particularly in the last area.

A large proportion of the people in the municipality have land. The rate varies according to zone, with a low of 25 per cent in the city, and a high of 83 per cent in the river zone, reporting that they have land in the rural area. The average for the road zone is 68 per cent. One might expect higher rates for the road zone because land was available for the taking when the road was opened in 1965. Further, holding land in this zone offers other opportunities for work, either along the road or in Itacoatiara itself; as well, supplies are more available than in the river zone. The lower proportion of landholders in the road zone may be explained by several factors. On the one hand, there is greater pressure from large landholders. On the other hand, the existence of employment alternatives (which are absent in the river zone), the possibility of cash transactions and speculative gains in a rapidly formaliz-ing land market, and poor soils can entice residents away from peasant farming.

Some expected relationships were not encountered in the analy-sis of the possession of land in relationship to a number of other variables. First, there is no relationship between possession of land and income. Of those with one minimum salary or less (N = 363), 58 per cent have land. With two salaries (N = 130), the figure is 57 per cent. With three or four salaries (N = 45), it is 69 per cent. With five to ten salaries (N = 27), it is 52 per cent. And with eleven or more (N = 6), it is 83 per cent. Statistically there is no relationship. Nor is there any relationship between previous migration and current ownership of land.

There are some indications from our data that the apparent stability of the population within the river zone and its relationship to the land are changing. The identifiable processes concern long-term secular trends involving general economic activity as well as more immediate processes brought about through the intervention of outside actors in the area.

EMPLOYMENT AND INCOME

Employment has shifted from the varzea to the terra firme. We asked the respondents about their work at present, five years ago, and ten years ago. Some 92 per cent of those involved in terra firme agriculture five years ago and 86 per cent of those involved ten years ago are still involved in it. The corresponding figures for varzea agriculture are 90 per cent and 83 per cent. Inversely, a full 97 per cent of those currently involved in varzea agriculture were doing precisely the same thing five years ago.

The comparable figure for those in terra firme agriculture is only 79 per cent; the other 21 per cent were involved in a variety of other activities, including 5 per cent in varzea agriculture, 6 per cent in construction, and 3 per cent in transport. It is relatively easy to move from non-agricultural jobs, construction, and transport, to terra firme agriculture, which now takes place mainly along the road.

There is not such an easy transference back to the varzea agriculture of the river zone. Less than 1 per cent came into varzea agriculture from either construction or transport. More importantly, whereas 6 per cent of those who were in varzea agriculture five years ago have now moved to terra firme, there is no movement back. (Over a ten-year period 2 per cent, or three individuals, moved to varzea agriculture.) The overall trend is clear: farmers leave varzea agriculture in the river zone and seldom go back. Nor is it likely that this trend will be reversed in the future, although the city apparently does not offer many attractive alternatives either.

The income of the respondents in the river zone is low in comparison to the incomes of those in the other two zones, as indicated in Table 18. Some 75 per cent of the respondents in the river zone receive the equivalent of one minimum salary or less, compared to 58 per cent in the road zone. The rural income figures would, however, appear significantly better if the value of subsistence production were added.

What also stands out is the relatively low income of heads of household in the city of Itacoatiara. Only 43 per cent of the city sample received two minimum salaries or above, and this implies real difficulties in survival. In contrast to the rural zones, it is somewhat more difficult to raise crops and to fish while living—and presumably working—in the city. These low incomes are particularly startling because the overall state development strategy in the area rests heavily on an urban-based plan centred on the wood industry. One might expect a higher level of general wealth than indicated in these data.

On looking further at the data on urban employment, we find that, despite the massive employment creation discussed in Chapter 3, a large percentage of the urban sample remains in the informal sector of the econ-

TABLE 18   *Income According to Municipal Zones of Itacoatiara*

Number of Minimum Salaries	Percentage			
	Road Zone	City	River Zone	Total
Less than 1	24	28	46	33
1	34	29	29	30
2	31	24	14	23
3-4	8	9	7	8
5-10	2	8	3	5
11 or more	1	2	1	1
Total	100	100	100	100

Note: N = 571

TABLE 19   *Employment of Respondents in the City of Itacoatiara*

Employment Categories	Percentage
Liberal professions	5
Banking	2
Public bureaucracy	20
Transportation	10
Commerce	25
Construction and industry	25
Rents or interest	2
Other	11
Total	100

Note: N = 136

TABLE 20   *Evaluation of Family Situation at Present Compared with Five Years Ago*

Evaluation	Percentage			
	Road Zone	City	River Zone	Total
Better	71	48	42	53
Same	16	20	18	18
Worse	13	32	40	29
Total	100	100	100	100

Note: N = 575

omy. That is, 52 per cent of the urban sample are employees, 1 per cent are employers, and 47 per cent are either autonomous urban workers or urban peons who do not have regular employment. Further, employment tends toward the lower end of the socio-economic scale.

Two points should be made concerning urban employment and the low level of income. First, there is, as one might expect, a transition from past rural employment to present urban employment. Of those currently working in construction and industry, 32 per cent were working in agriculture ten years ago. Of those currently working in commerce, 27 per cent were working in agriculture ten years ago. Of those currently working in transport, 14 per cent were working in agriculture ten years ago. Second, not expected but very important, are the relative growth rates of the different forms of employment. Ten years ago, 38 per cent of those involved in urban employment were in construction and industry, compared with 25 per cent today. Some 20 per cent were involved in commerce, compared with 25 per cent today. Most importantly, whereas 9 per cent, or twelve individuals, worked for some branch of government ten years ago, today the public bureaucracy constitutes 20 per cent, or twenty-nine persons of the urban sample (Table 19). Thus, whereas there has been a relative decline in industrial employment, in spite of expansion in the wood-processing sector, the public bureaucracy has experienced explosive growth in relative terms.

There is awareness among the sample in both the city and the river zone that things have not improved substantially. We asked whether the family situation is better or worse than five years ago; the data displayed in Table 20 show gains in good part balanced by losses in the river zone and city.

A series of serious floods in the five years preceding the time of the survey may account in part for the outmigration, low income, and dissatisfaction of the riverine population. In the city the evaluation should be better because of the availability of services (education, health, water, and electricity) and the employment opportunities. But a process of proletarianization or marginalization is apparent, with little quality urban employment and as yet little change in attitudes. We will expand on this later in this chapter.

AGRICULTURAL CREDIT AND PROPERTY TITLES

As indicated in chapters 2 and 3, agricultural credit was very important at the time of the survey. Whether modern bank credit replaced traditional sources is another matter.

In fact, 40 per cent of those who had received crop loans from bank sources in 1980–1981 had also obtained credit from traditional sources. Of those involved in agriculture (N = 367), 33 per cent had been granted bank financing for one or more crops in the preceding twelve months. Further, in 1981 some 38 per cent had been promised financing. However, not all of the respondents with financing were able to repay the credit they had received with the sale of their crops. In the road zone, where credit largely financed the planting of manioc for the local and Manaus market, a vast majority—82 per cent of credit holders—considered themselves able to repay their debts. In the river zone, 75 per cent of the credit was for jute and malva destined for southern Brazilian markets. In 1981 these crops were affected by low official prices and cheap imports, and only 26 per cent of respondents thought that they would be able to repay their debts with their crop. Many of these debts have not been paid off, and have, in fact, increased dramatically because of rising interest rates and monetary adjustment. Overdue credit is a potentially disruptive issue with regard to land ownership, although the banks seem unwilling or unable to foreclose on the debts.

Another complex topic relating to the holding of land, particularly in the river zone, is the possession of land titles. There is a variety of documents of varying value. The most important is the definitive title provided by INCRA or ITERAM in their respective jurisdictions. Interestingly, a strong relationship exists between income and possession of the definitive title, as indicated in Table 21.

Those with more money are much more likely to possess the definitive title. Although the direction of the relationship is not known for certain, it is likely that those who are better off are consequently better educated or more knowledgeable. They realize the importance of obtaining the definitive title and are able to make the necessary interventions to ensure continuing claim to the land. This financial/legal relationship also suggests that a process of selectivity is emerging, whereby wealthier, more astute landowners interested in long-term investment are increasing the value of their land. The possession of the definitive title adds to the value of the land and facilitates its sale. As yet this process is taking place primarily in the road areas. Only a minority of landholders (15 per cent) possess the definitive title. This varies by region, with a high of 31 per cent holding title in the road zone and a low of 4 per cent in the river zone. Of the other available forms of property documentation, registration in the INCRA cadaster and the Occupation Licence (LO) are the most common; only 1 per cent in the river zone hold either of these documents, in contrast to 11 per cent in the road zone.

TABLE 21   *Relationship between Income and Definitive Land Title*

Number of Minimum Salaries	Percentage with Definitive Title
Less than 1	8
1	11
2	20
3-4	27
5-10	29
11 or more	40

Note: N = 339

It might be noted, as reported in Chapter 3, that INCRA and ITERAM gave priority to the road zone in their titling programs. Even so, it seems important to stress the low degree of importance placed on land titles by those in the river zone, because it not only indicates an attitude toward the land for its use value (rather than as a commodity) but also suggests problems if there is increased pressure on the land linked to or independent of the indebtedness arising from agricultural credit. Whether this does happen and what its results might be depends on caboclo awareness and willingness to resist pressure.

COMMUNITY ORGANIZATION AND PROBLEMS

As noted in Chapter 2, there is a union of rural workers (STR) whose purpose is to defend the interests of the caboclos. It has had its ups and downs but, at the time of the survey, a high percentage of our sample indicated that they belonged to it. Membership varied from 41 per cent in the road zone to 46 per cent in the river zone. If the union were strong, the land holders could deal with their problems concerning indebtedness and documents through the union; unfortunately, it is not strong.

Also, the Church is extremely active in the municipality and has energetically promoted the formation of the basic Christian communities. In the road area, some 40 per cent of respondents reported that they belonged to the communities, whereas in the river zone, where the local Church is very active, an impressive 62 per cent reported membership. (In the city, which was not worked intensively by the Church, only 19 per cent reported that they belonged to the communities.) It should also be noted that there is a strong correlation between membership in the STR and the communities. Some 51 per cent of those in the communities belong to the union; or, the other way around, 70 per cent of the members of the union belong to the communities. This result is not unexpected because the Church has been active in promoting both and the communities have often acted as the seedbeds for the formation of the union. To some degree, then, the people do possess organizations whereby they might work to defend their interests, should the pressure on the land increase.

Based on data concerning the perception of problems facing the respondent and his family, it is difficult to be sanguine about the capability of the population, especially in the river zone, to defend its interests. Generally the respondents could identify problems in response to an open-ended question (88 per cent reported a problem). However, the specific problems reported in response to this question varied greatly, as indicated in Table 22.

The majority reported a high rate of general difficulties, but most failed to articulate a clear hierarchy of problems. In the river zone, there was an appropriately high response for low prices for agricultural goods, but a low response for problems due to action or inaction by the three levels of government. Surprisingly, only 12 per cent of city respondents reported problems attributable to the three levels of government in spite of the disparity

TABLE 22   *The Major Problem Reported as Facing Respondent and Family*

	Percentage			
Problem	Road Zone	City	River Zone	Total
General difficulties	39	61	67	57
Specific shortcomings attributed to government and politics	38	12	9	19
Health problems	8	15	4	8
Low prices for agricultural products	1	1	15	6
Lack of work	1	2	1	1
Lack of land and/or housing	9	2	1	4
Low salaries	1	8	2	4
Crime and social problems	2	1	—	1
Environmental problems	2	1	2	1
Total	101	103	101	101

Note: N = 510

TABLE 23   *Entity Which Should Resolve Problem*

	Percentage			
Entity Noted	Road Zone	City	River Zone	Total
Person himself	10	17	14	14
Community	18	13	24	18
Patrão	3	4	1	2
Governments	49	28	33	36
Sindicato (STR) or co-operative	3	1	3	2
Church	1	—	1	1
Only God	16	35	25	25
No solution	1	4	—	1
Total	101	102	101	99

Note: N = 510

between visibility and achievements of public entities. The 15 per cent reporting health problems in the city seems high, particularly in comparison with the figures for the other two zones. It may suggest a serious problem of marginalization and poor diet because the salaries are low and city dwellers have limited opportunities for subsistence agriculture, fishing, and hunting. At the same time, the supply of fresh foods in the city has not diversified and price inflation has affected fish in particular.

What stands out, most definitely, is the very different pattern of response for the road zone, where a large proportion of respondents could indicate specific deficiencies due to governments as well as a lack of land and housing. The same pattern pertains in the data reported in Table 23, which concerns who should resolve the problems.

Of particular importance in Table 23 is the very high response by those in the road zone for the governments to resolve their problems; this corresponds to the responses reported in Table 22. Also of note is the relatively high figure in the river zone for community responsibility—a priority of the Church—and the low 1 per cent for the Church itself. It would seem that the Church has been successful in having the people, especially in this area, look to the community rather than to the Church. Somewhat surprising, but not without basis, is the low responsibility attributed to the Sindicato. Apparently the rural population, not to mention the urban population, expects little from the union. What is most startling is the very high figure for "only God." In the river zone, the 25 per cent is high because it means they do not perceive a solution. Here, however, one needs to recognize that extreme floods, of which an unprecedented series visited the area in the 1970s, are "acts of God" beyond the control of man. More disturbing is the 39 per cent given by the city dwellers for "only God" and "no solution." It would seem that with their inability to specify problems, as indicated in Table 22, and their fatalism as indicated in Table 23, they have real problems. In contrast, the respondents in the road zone face many problems, including pressure on the land, but they attribute responsibility to the government—which can take action—as well as noting specific problems. There is much to explain in this pattern.

In the road zone, settlement is newer and more intentional. The road was completed in 1965 by using a great deal of labour. After its completion, some workers chose to remain in the road area rather than go to or remain in the city, let alone the river zone. Others were subsequently attracted. Since coming to this area they have seen an increase in large holdings, a role for government which is active in extension and other projects, including expanding and paving the road, and they are aware of options because the road connects the first and second cities of the state of Amazonas. A process of selection is operative; these people are more aware because they have been exposed to more, are under more pressure on their land, and perceive other opportunities. In contrast, the residents in the river zone and even in the city have yet to experience this process.

The data reviewed in this chapter indicate that there are different perceptions of problems and solutions among the various populations of the municipality. Those in the river zone and the city are still very much within a caboclo mentality. The residents in the city apparently have the worst of all worlds because, in their move from the rural area to the city, they have found bare subsistence living and little opportunity for upward mobility. They must cope through the large informal employment sector and low wages. The biggest growth in the city has been in the public sector, which employs 20 per cent of city respondents. In the rural areas, the situation of the residents is becoming problematic because of indebtedness, although there is still room for flexibility. There is a trend away from the river zone, and low incomes, floods, and lack of infrastructure will surely keep this process going. Although the residents in the river zone do belong to the union and communities, they do not have a very high level of awareness. At the time of the study, the urban workers lacked a viable union to defend their poorly defined interests. Along the road, the responses are different but the question is whether the degree of awareness and the presence of organizations are sufficient to confront the increasing pressure on the land which these data seem to suggest.

CONCLUSION

This book is a description and analysis of the process of change taking place in one municipality of the Middle Amazon. Itacoatiara was rather typical of a site of old settlement on the main course of the Amazon River. Located below the confluence of the Amazon and Madeira rivers, it served as an entrepot for the surrounding territory. The local society was reasonably stable and organized on the basis of traditional patron-client relationships. The basis of local subsistence was varzea agriculture with fish as a crucial element of the daily diet. The terra firme hinterland is characterized by poor soils and thus did not attract settlers from outside, as has been the case elsewhere, particularly in the southern and eastern parts of the Amazon. The key characteristics of Itacoatiara which make it particularly interesting for study are its long history of settlement and its road link to the state capital, Manaus. It differs from most of the other areas of the Amazon because no official colonization scheme has been implemented and, due to the low quality of the soils, there has been no explosion of settlement causing tensions and conflict that pit posseiros, Indians, and large landowners against one another in violent confrontations.

Yet Itacoatiara has indeed gone through a process of change which threatens the nature of traditional landholding and caboclo life. As in other parts of the Amazon, modern Brazil has reached Itacoatiara with impressive force which can only be expected to increase. New actors include large out-of-state landowners, the lumber industry in its modern incarnation, and a variety of state offices and agencies. Inclusion in modern Brazil seems completely irreversible because the lumber industry will continue to expand inasmuch as Itacoatiara's location allows logs to be floated the length of the Solimoes and the Madeira, and lagoons upriver in the municipality serve as storage ponds. Growth in the lumber industry between 1981 and November 1985, when one member of the team revisited Itacoatiara, was impressive in terms of the expansion of the Atlantic Veneer (now called Carolina) factory and the general community view of Itacoatiara as an industrial centre. The city has now reached a level of infrastructure—such as roads, electricity, telecommunications, and banking facilities—which ensures that it will continue to grow. Even the outlying districts, for example, are now linked by telephone and the installed electrical capacity was doubled between 1981 and 1986. With its paved road link to Manaus and with plans to put a bridge over at least one of the two Urubú River crossings, the city will be increasingly interdependent on Manaus and the rest of Brazil. What are the implications for the life of the people in this stage of Brazilian development?

In the rural area, it is most likely that there will be a continuing and increasing process of tenure polarization as large enterprises expand livestock production and agriculture, particularly in the road zone but also in the river zone. This polarization will be less visible than in other parts of the Amazon, such as southern Pará and Mato Grosso, due to the much lower quality of lands in Itacoatiara. This process will also be slowed due to the fact that the river zone is too disaggregated to be easily integrated into larger enterprises. With the process of mapping, titling, and transfer, an awareness of land constraints should develop beyond that noted for the road zone residents in our survey.

Increasingly, land will be valued less for its productivity and more as a commodity, as real estate. The caboclos can sell it or hold on and try to improve it with inputs which will require some capital and a more coordinated government program than exists at present. In any case, land is gradually becoming a commodity without the radical shift which has led to serious conflict in other parts of the Amazon. There are cases of conflict in Itacoatiara as well, but these are as yet minor and promise to remain so in the near future. Depletion of natural resources, especially fish, specialization in lieu of traditional diversification, and increased reliance on the terra firme may ultimately prove to be a greater threat to the rural population than land acquisition by large enterprise.

Three characteristics of the process of change or development are of particular importance in moderating conflict in Itacoatiara. The first has been frequently mentioned: the poor quality of land in the terra firme hinterland, so that great numbers of dynamic settlers from outside the area have not moved in nor are they likely to do so, as much of the area has now been mapped and titled. The pressure, then, will not be based on these dynamic outsiders with nowhere else to go, but rather on the caboclo with his somewhat less active or dynamic style. The second concerns the early formation of groups or movements whose purpose is to enable the caboclos to organize and defend their interests. The principal reason for this early formation is the active presence of the Catholic Church in the municipality, which pursues strategies of change similar to those elsewhere in Brazil where threats have been greater. The caboclos, then, have basic Christian communities and a rural union which at least in form allow them to confront threats. With these frameworks, negotiation is possible and conflict can be structured, thereby decreasing the possibility for violence. Third, there has been little real change in the local political elite in Itacoatiara. External actors have been added to the political and economic configuration, but the old elite of traders and landowners who also control the local government has not been replaced. This suggests that the elite continues to deal with the caboclo population in more or less traditional patterns. In addition, while an infusion of new actors has appeared at the top, largely from the outside, there has been little political mobility from the bottom of local society. In these ways, contestation and polarization have been minimized and conflict is fairly limited, given the extent of change in the industrial base and the transformation taking place on the land and probable changes in the caboclos' life styles.

The facility with which young people can move to Manaus without breaking links with their families in Itacoatiara is of particular significance in the lack of political mobility from the bottom, or even middle, to the top. From our analysis of the data on income and employment in

Itacoatiara it seems clear that there are simply too few opportunities for those who are young, talented, and ambitious. They must leave for professional training and are unlikely to return. The upper level of business is monopolized by the traditional elite and is not sufficiently dynamic to justify the investment of scarce capital. Jobs in construction and industry, as well as in transportation, are at the minimum salary, if not less. And the bureaucracy has expanded predominantly at the lower levels such as teachers, lesser bureaucrats, and petty city employees. In the absence of active and ambitious leadership, there is little likelihood of polarization and conflict.

What are the possibilities of a different direction or orientation to the process of change in Itacoatiara? The industrial growth and the slow but sure transformation of agriculture are irreversible. Which actors can give a different orientation, and how? In the rural areas there are few real issues. In the river zone, ownership is ambiguous and titling is slow, but so far there is little pressure. Although many caboclos are heavily indebted, it seems unlikely that the banks will foreclose and take over the land. Along the road there is more pressure, but mapping and titling are regularizing the process of land sale. Some people will undoubtedly lose their land, but will probably be paid for it and are unlikely to resist violently as in other parts of the Amazon. The overall lack of concern and commitment on the part of the caboclos is illustrated by the cyclical ups and downs of the rural union. The caboclos have an organization for their defence but, since its founding in 1972, it has seen at least two periods of decay. It has been most dynamic when a particularly serious issue arose for the caboclos, such as indebtedness. Since 1981, however, because the banks have not foreclosed, the union has fallen into a state of decay and its members have stopped paying their dues. It would seem that it cannot rely on awareness and commitment among the caboclos, and thus the leaders tend to bicker and to allow themselves to be co-opted. In the past the union has relied on the Church for orientation and support, and today it continues to rely on the Church as well as on the Confederation located in Manaus. It seems unlikely that, without another dramatic issue, the rural union will become revitalized.

The most dramatic events, on the part of lower-sector organization and militancy, were the taking over of the owner-controlled union of woodworkers and two strikes in mid- and late-1985. These moves were supported by the Church and also required outside assistance, again from Manaus. Despite the continuing low level of awareness and commitment on the part of urban workers, it was possible to hold strikes which were mildly successful. The indigenous leadership admits that it is weak and incohesive. But the dynamic growth of the lumber industry, the concentration of workers, and the serious situation in working conditions and wages may lead to greater awareness and a stronger union. At present, this is the most promising area for change and, as a fairly broad degree of support for the strikers existed at the time of the second strike in November 1985, it seems possible that events of this sort will increase the present low level of awareness.

The key actors setting the parameters for change are undoubtedly the local government and the Church. The local government remains
under the control of the same local business elite; now, however, they have
changed parties and engage in more internal bickering because of the possibilities for manoeuvring allowed by the recent liberalization in Brazilian
national, state, and local politics. All indications are that this local elite will
endure because none of the new, external actors would be interested in changing it and, as yet, the lower classes do not have sufficient cohesiveness or
strength to do so.

The Catholic Church, as has become clear, not only supports
the formation of organizations for the mass of the population, but also provides
a variety of resources for general mobilization and awareness. It should be
noted, however, that the Church has been very weak in forming communities in the road zone and there are few communities and little general support in the city. Thus, in precisely the most dynamically changing areas, the
Church, for a variety of strategic reasons, has not promoted the formation
of those organizations which can serve as a basis for further development of
class-based organizations. However, its power can be great and, for this
reason, the local government has actively attempted to co-opt communities,
to wrest them from the Church and rely on them at election time.

In sum, there are new actors, change will continue at its slow
pace, and there are indications that benefits may be more widely shared in
the future. The caboclos strongly resist change of any kind, but they cannot
avoid having to adapt to their changing environment. There are some indications that this adaptation is gradually taking place.

REFERENCES CITED

Barbira-Scazzocchio, Françoise, ed., 1980 *Land, People and Planning in Contemporary Amazonia*. Cambridge: Centre of Latin American Studies, Occasional Publication No. 3.

Barrow, C.J., 1985 The Development of the Varzeas (Floodlands) of Brazilian Amazonia. In *Change in the Amazon Basin*, Vol. 1, John Hemming, ed. pp. 108–28. Manchester: Manchester University Press.

Benchimol, Samuel, 1985 Population Changes in the Brazilian Amazon. In *Change in the Amazon Basin*, Vol. 2, John Hemming, ed. pp. 37–50. Manchester: Manchester University Press.

Bourne, Richard, 1978 The Manaus Pendulum. *Geographical Magazine* 50(4): 258–63.

Bruneau, Thomas C., 1986 The Catholic Church and Basic Christian Communities. In *Religion and Political Conflict in Latin America*. Daniel H. Levine, ed. pp. 106–24. Chapel Hill: University of North Carolina Press.

Bunker, Stephen G., 1981 The Impact of Deforestation on Peasant Communities in the Médio Amazonas of Brazil. *Studies in Third World Societies* 13: 45–60.

———. 1985 *Underdeveloping the Amazon*. Urbana and Chicago: University of Illinois Press.

Cardoso, Fernando H. and G. Muller, 1977 *Amazônia: Expansão do Capitalismo*. São Paulo: Brasiliense.

Carvalho, Murilo, 1980 *Sangue da Terra; A Luta Armada no Campo*. São Paulo: Brasil Debates.

Centro de Assistência Gerencial à Pequena e Média Empresa do Estado do Amazonas (CEAG-AM), no date *Cadastro Industrial do Amazonas 1978/79*. Manaus.

Conferencia Nacional dos Bispos do Brasil (CNBB), 1977 *Pastoral da Terra: Posse e Conflitos*. São Paulo: Edições Paulinas.

Cooperativa Mista Agropecuária de Itacoatiara. 1980 Relatorio de Atividades 1980. Itacoatiara. (mimeograph).

Denevan, William M., 1984 Ecological Heterogeneity and Horizontal Zonation of Agriculture in the Amazon Flood Plain. In *Frontier Expansion in Amazonia*. Marianne Schmink and Charles H. Wood, eds. pp. 311–36. Gainesville: University of Florida Press.

Departamento Nacional da Produçao Mineral (DNPM), 1976 *Projeto RADAM BRASIL*, Vol. 10, Folha SA. 21–Santarém. Rio de Janeiro.

Fearnside, Philip M., 1985 Environmental Change and Deforestation in the Brazilian Amazon. In *Change in the Amazon Basin*, Vol. 1, John Hemming, ed. pp. 70–90. Manchester: Manchester University Press.

Foweraker, Joe, 1981 *The Struggle for Land: A Political Economy of the Pioneer Frontier in Brazil from 1930 to the Present Day*. Cambridge: Cambridge University Press.

Hemming, John, ed. 1985a *Change in the Amazon Basin. Vol. 1, Man's Impact on Forests and Rivers*. Manchester: Manchester University Press.

———. 1985b *Change in the Amazon Basin. Vol. 2, The Frontier After a Decade of Colonization*. Manchester: Manchester University Press.

Higbee, E.C., 1945 The River is the Plow. *Scientific Monthly* 60: 405–16.

Hiraoka, Mario, 1985a Changing Floodplain Livelihood Patterns in the Peruvian Amazon. *Tsukuba Studies in Human Geography*, IX(3): 243–75.

———. 1985b Floodplain Farming in the Peruvian Amazon. *Geographical Review of Japan* 58 (Ser. B), 1: 1–23.

———. 1985c Mestizo Subsistence in Riparian Amazônia. *National Geographic Research*, Spring 1985: 236–46.

Ianni, Octavio, 1979 *Colonização e Contra-Reforma Agraria na Amazônia*. Petropolis: Editora Vozes.

Instituto Brasileiro de Geografia e Estadistica (IBGE)
——— . 1970a *Censo Agropecuário*. Rio de Janeiro.
——— . 1970b *Censo Demográfico*. Rio de Janeiro.
——— . 1970c *Censo dos Servicos*. Rio de Janeiro.
——— . 1970d *Censo Comercial*. Rio de Janeiro.
——— . 1975 *Censo Agropecuário*. Rio de Janeiro.
——— . 1980a *Censo Agropecuário*. Rio de Janeiro.
——— . 1980b *Censo Agropecuário*. Manual do Recensador. Rio de Janeiro.
——— . 1980c *Censo Demográfico*. Rio de Janeiro.
——— . 1980d *Censo dos Servicos*. Rio de Janeiro.
——— . 1980e *Censo Comercial*. Rio de Janeiro

Junk, Wolfgang Johannes, 1983 As Aguas da Região Amazonica. In *Amazônia: Desenvolvimento, Integração e Ecologia*. Eneas Salati et al., eds. pp. 45–100. São Paulo: Brasiliense.

Lima, R.R., 1956 A Agricultura nas Varzeas do Estuario do Amazonas. Belém: Instituto Agronomico do Norte, Boletin Técnio, No. 33.

Mahar, Dennis, 1976 Fiscal Incentives for Regional Development: A Case Study of the Western Amazon Basin. *Journal of Interamerican Studies and World Affairs*. 18(3): 357–78.
——— . 1979 *Frontier Development Policy in Brazil: A Study of Amazonia*. New York: Praeger.

Malafaia, M.A. et al., 1969 Destaque sobre a Cultura do Arroz no Estado do Amazonas. Manaus: Ministério da Agricultura (mimeograph).

Mendonça Leite, Lúcia Hermelinda de, 1981 "Comunidades: Caminando se Abre Caminhos." M.A. thesis, IBRADES, Rio de Janeiro.

Moran, Emilio F., 1974 The Adaptive System of the Amazonian Caboclo. In *Man in the Amazon*. Charles Wagley, ed. pp. 136–59. Gainesville, Fla.: University of Florida Press.
——— . 1981 *Developing the Amazon*. Bloomington: Indiana University Press.

Moran, Emilio F., ed. 1983 *The Dilemma of Amazonian Development*. Boulder: Westview Press.

Neto, Miranda, 1979 *O Dilema da Amazônia*. Petropolis: Editora Vozes.

Nordin, C.F. and R.H. Meade, 1982 Deforestation and Increased Flooding of the Upper Amazon. *Science* 215: 426–27.

Oliveira, Adélia Engrácia de, 1983 Ocupação Humana. In *Amazônia: Desenvolvimento, Integração e Ecologia*. Eneas Salati et al. pp. 144–327. São Paulo: Brasiliense.

Parker, Eugene P., 1981 "Cultural Ecology and Change: A Caboclo Várzea Community in the Brazilian Amazon." Ph.D. dissertation, University of Colorado.

Parker, Eugene P., ed., 1985 The Amazon Caboclo: Historical and Contemporary Perspectives. *Studies in Third World Societies*, No. 32.

Pompermayer, Malori José, 1979 "The State and the Frontier in Brazil: A Case Study of the Amazon." Ph.D. dissertation, Stanford University.

Potter, Gerald Lee, 1975 "Anthropogenic Climate Modification: Modeling the Removal of the Tropical Rain Forest." Ph.D. dissertation, University of California at Los Angeles.

Ross, Eric B., 1978 The Evolution of the Amazon Peasantry. *Journal of Latin American Studies* 10(2): 193–218.

Sawyer, Donald R., 1984 Frontier Expansion and Retraction in Brazil. In *Frontier Expansion in Amazonia*. Marianne Schmink and Charles H. Wood, eds. pp. 180–203. Gainesville: University of Florida Press.

Schmink, Marianne and Charles H. Wood, eds., 1984 *Frontier Expansion in Amazonia*. Gainesville: University of Florida Press.

Secretaria de Estado da Coordenação do Planejamento (SEPLAN), 1980a Prosposição de uma Politica de Desenvolvimento Urbano Regional. Manaus: Estado do Amazonas.

———. 1980b Diagnóstico da 8a Sub-Região; Versão Preliminar. Manaus: Estado do Amazonas.

Skillings, Robert and Nils O. Tcheyan, 1979 Economic Development Prospects of the Amazon Region of Brazil. Washington, D.C.: The Johns Hopkins University, Occasional Paper No. 9 of the Center of Brazilian Studies.

Smith, Nigel J.H., 1980 Anthrosols and Human Carrying Capacity in Amazonia. *Annals of the Association of American Geographers* 70: 553–66.

———. 1981 *Man, Fishes and the Amazon*. New York: Columbia University Press.

———. 1982 *Rainforest Corridors*. Berkeley: University of California Press.

Souza Martins, José de, 1980 *Expropriação e Violéncia*. São Paulo: Hucitec.

———. 1981 *Os Camponeses e a Politica no Brasil*. Petropolis: Editora Vozes.

———. 1984 The State and the Militarization of the Agrarian Question in Brazil. In *Frontier Expansion in Amazonia*. Marianne Schmink and Charles H. Wood, eds. pp. 463–90. Gainesville: University of Florida Press.

Sternberg, Hilgard O'Reilly, 1956 "A Agua e o Homem na Várzea do Careiro." Ph.D. dissertation, Universidade do Brasil, Rio de Janeiro.

Superintendência do Desenvolvimento da Amazônia (SUDAM) 1970 Relatório Preliminar de Desenvolvimento Integrado: Município de Itacoatiara. Manaus: SUDAM.

Sweet, David, 1974 "A Rich Realm of Nature Destroyed: The Middle Amazon Valley (1640–1750)." Ph.D. dissertation, University of Wisconsin, Madison.

Velho, Octavio Guilherme, 1979 *Capitalismo Autoritario e Campesinato*. São Paulo: Difel.

Wagley, Charles, ed., 1974 *Man in the Amazon*. Gainesville: University Presses of Florida.

———. 1984 Foreword. In *Frontier Expansion in Amazonia*. Marianne Schmink and Charles H. Wood, eds. pp. ix–xiv. Gainesville: University of Florida Press.

Weinstein, Barbara, 1980 "Prosperity without Development: The Paraense Elite and the Amazon Rubber Boom (1850–1920)." Ph.D. dissertation, Yale University.